FROM THE BIG HOUSE TO YOUR HOUSE

Cooking in prison

With

Ceyma Bina, Tina Cornelius,
Barbara Holder, Celeste Johnson,
Trenda Kemmerer, and Louanne Larson

From The Big House To Your House – Cooking In Prison
Copyright © 2010
Ceyma Bina, Tina Cornelius,
Barbara Holder, Celeste Johnson,
Trenda Kemmerer, and Louanne Larson

All Rights Reserved.

Published by:
The Justice Institute
PO Box 68911
Seattle, WA 98168
www.justicedenied.org
info@justicedenied.org

First edition, December 2010
Second printing

ISBN: 1453644318
ISBN-13: 978-1453644317

Special Notes:

TDCJ is the Texas Department of Criminal Justice

Units are Texas Department of Criminal Justice operated prisons

As of October 2010, all information in the "Did You Know?" is referring to the Mountain View Unit (women's prison) unless specifically noted otherwise.

Dedication

To Nancy Hall (Celeste Johnson's mother)

You worked long and hard so that an "idea" we had over two years ago would finally become a reality. In this dismal setting we see much darkness; yet you continue to show us the stars. It is impossible to count the many incarcerated women that you unselfishly help. It is from your guidance, commitment, and support that we dedicate this book to you. You are truly our blessing and we love you and appreciate you.

Donation of Proceeds

All proceeds from sales of *From The Big House To Your House* are being donated by the book's six authors to The Justice Institute to aid in its work on behalf of aiding the wrongly convicted and promoting awareness of wrongful convictions. The Justice Institute publishes *Justice Denied – the magazine for the wrongly convicted*, and its website is www.justicedenied.org.

Table Of Contents

Preface
I – Feast In A Bag 1
    Almost Teriyaki Soup 2
    Bacon Sandwich 2
    BBQ Beef Sandwich 3
    Bean and Pork Burritos 3
    Bean Burritos 4
    Beef Taquitos 4
    Beef Tips & Rice 5
    Beef Vegetable Soup 5
    Buttered Noodles 6
    Cheeseburger 6
    Cheesy Potato Tacos 7
    Cheesy Rice Casserole 7
    Chicken & Cheese Enchiladas 8
    Chicken & Dumplings 8
    Chicken & Rice 9
    Chicken & Rice Soup 9
    Chicken & Lemon Pepper Rice 10
    Chicken/Bacon Tacos 10
    Chili Cheese Burritos 11
    Chili Cheese Burritos, Two! 11
    Chili Cheese Dogs 12
    Chili Pie 12
    Chimichangas 13
    Chopa's 13
    Chorizo Tacos 14
    Country Rice 14
    Delightful Tuna Nachos 15
    Deluxe Mexican Nachos 15
    Delightful Tuna Nachos, Two! 16
    Enchiladas 16
    Enticing Enchiladas 17
    Gumbo 17
    Fast & Delicious Burrito 18
    Fish Stix 19

Hash Browns	20
Holiday Fruit Salad	20
Hot Ham & Cheese Sandwich	21
Hot Tuna Casserole	21
Hot Wingless Wraps	22
Indian Rice	22
Jalapeno Poppers	23
Mackerel/Sardines in Rice	23
Mackerel with no Cook Tomato Sauce	24
Meaty Nachos	24
Menudo	25
Mexican Pizza	25
Mexican Rice	26
More Than Cheese Quesadillas	26
Nachos Deluxe	27
Oriental Rice	28
Pasta Parmesan	28
Pasta Salad	29
Pasta Salad, Two!	29
Pazones	30
Peanut Rice	30
Pizza Fold	31
Po' Man's Burrito	31
Potato Soup	32
Potluck Soup	32
Punk Rock Tacos	33
Red Beans and Rice	33
Sardine Dip	34
Sardines & Rice	34
Sausage Burritos	35
Scalloped Potatoes	35
Shish Kabobs With Rice	36
"Skin Of The Pig" Burrito	36
Southwestern Style Chicken Quesadillas	37
Spicy Potato Burrito	37
Spicy Gumbo	38
Stuffed Potato	38
Spicy Potato Salad	39
Stuffed Ham	39

Stuffed Peppers..40
Summer Sausage Sandwich 40
Stuffed Sausage 41
Sweet-N-Sour Sandwiches..41
Super Layered Nachos 42
Sweet & Sour Tuna Salad 42
Tamales 43
Tomato Soup 43
Tangy & Crunchy Tuna Salad 44
Traditional Tuna Sandwich With Zest..44
Tuna Ball 45
Tuna Boat 45
Tuna Tacos 46
Tuna Wraps 46
Tuna Wraps, Two!...47
Zesty Tuna Tacos...47
Yummy Mexican Tacos 48
Zesty/Tangy Nachos 48
II - Snacks, Dips and More...49
All Purpose Cheese Sauce...50
All Round Dip 50
BBQ Bean Dip..51
Bean Dip..51
Butter Pickles 52
Cheese Dip 52
Chipolte Mayo 53
Creamy Butter Beans 53
Creamy Choconilla Drink 53
Dip-n-Lick 54
Faux Sangria' 54
Guacamole...55
Homemade Salsa 55
Italian Ice...56
Mackerel Soaks 56
Mexican Snacks..57
Munch'n Mix...57
Peach Habenero Salsa 58
Pin Wheels..58
Popcorn Ball 59

Popcorn Krispies	59
Potato Salad	60
Rainbow Slushies	60
Ranch Dip/Sandwich Spread	61
Relish	61
Sandwich Mustard Dressing	61
Sandwich Dressings	62
Simple Rice	62
Soy Sauce	62
Spanish Rice	63
Spanish Rice, Two!	63
Sweet-N-Spicy Rice	64
Sweet & Sour Pickles	64
Sweet & Tangy Mustard	65
Sweet Mayo	65
Sweet Rice Casserole	66
1001 Island Dressing	66
III – For The Sweet Tooth	**67**
Almond Joyous Cake	68
Any Flavor Pudding	68
Apple Streudel	69
Banana Pudding	69
Banana Nut Bread	70
Black Cherry Delight	70
Banana Pudding, Two!	71
Banana Split Cake	71
Basic Cheesecake	72
Basic Cheesecake, Two!	73
Birthday Surprise	73
Black Cherry Cheese Cake	74
Caramel Latte	74
Black Forest Cake	75
Brownie Cake	75
Blondie Brownie	76
Chocolate Candy Cluster	76
Chocolate Cheese Cake	77
Chocolate Covered Cherries	77
Chocolate Crème Pizza	78
Chocolate Lovers Dream …With Ice Cream	78

Chocolate & Mint Cookies 79
Chocolate & Peanut Butter Bowl 79
Chocolate Nutty Bar Cake 80
Choc–O–Holic Delights 80
Chocolate Peanut Butter Cake 81
Chocolate Peanut Butter Cups 81
Chocolate Pudding 82
Chocolate Rice Crispy Cake 82
Chuckles 83
Coconut Cake 83
Coconut Chocolate Cake 84
Confetti Cake 84
Chocolate Cookie Cake 85
Cookie Twists 85
Death By Chocolate 86
Delectable Brownies 86
Fantasy Fudge Cake 87
Frosted Shredded Wheat Surprise 87
Fruit Cakes 88
Girly Scout Cookies 88
Grasshoppers 89
Halloween Cake 89
Ice Cream Cheese Cake 90
Ice Cream Chocolate Crunch 90
Ice Cream Parfait 91
Ice Cream Pudding Cone 91
Ice Cream Sandwich Cakes 92
Lemon Coconut Bars 92
Melt In Your Mouth Frosting 93
Milk & Honey Surprises 93
Mini Ice Cream Sandwiches 94
Mini Popcorn Balls 94
Mint Chocolate Cake 95
Mint Cookie Chocolate Drops 95
Mint Delights 96
Mississippi Mud Brownies 96
Mississippi Mud Cakes 97
Oatmeal/Peanut Butter Cookies 97
Peach Pie Crunch 98
Peanut Butter Brownie Cups 98

Peanut Butter Granola Balls 99
Peanut Butter & Jelly Pie – The Old Standby 99
Quick Cheesecake for One 100
Real Strawberry Cheesecake 100
Red Apple & Banana Cheese Cake 101
Smores..101
Strawberry-Vanilla Cheesecake...102
Swindler's Cups..102
Tira Misu Chocolate...103
Tree Barks 103
Very Berry Cobbler Parfait 104
When The Lock Box Is Empty Cake 104

V – Prison Lingo 105
Books for Sale..112

Preface

Welcome to cooking in prison!

This book is the result of our cooking experiences while confined at the Mountain View Unit, a woman's prison in Gatesville, Texas. We met and bonded in the G-3 dorm housing only prisoners with a sentence in excess of 50 years. While there isn't much freedom to be found when incarcerated, using the commissary to cook what YOU want offers a wonderful avenue for creativity and enjoyment! We hope these recipes will ignite your taste buds as well as spark your imagination to explore unlimited creations of your own! We encourage you to make substitutions to your individual tastes and/or availability of ingredients. We are confident that you will enjoy the liberty found in creating a home-felt comfort during unfortunate times.

Happy Cooking!

Barbara, Celeste, Ceyma, Louanne, Tina, and Trenda

ALMOST TERIYAKI SOUP

1 package beef or chicken soup	1/4 cup salsa verde chips (crushed)
1 teaspoon coffee (instant dried)	1 tablespoons jalapeno chips (crushed)
1 package jalapeno peppers (seeded and diced) (desired amount)	4 tablespoons jalapeno cheese (heaping)

Cook noodles. Place hot water in coffee cup (about one inch from bottom) and add coffee and 1/2 package seasoning mix. Stir and add to drained noodles. Add peppers, cheese, chips, and mix thoroughly. Serve with crackers or chips.
Serves: 2

> **DID YOU KNOW?** By a 5 to 4 vote, the Supreme Court said young people serving life prison terms must have "a meaningful opportunity to obtain release" if they haven't killed their victims.
> *The Associated Press* by Mark Sherman – May 18, 2010

BACON SANDWICH

1/2 bag pork skins	1 tablespoon salad dressing
1 tablespoon jalapeno cheese	2 slices bread

On one slice of bread spread jalapeno cheese. On the other slice, spread salad dressing. Layer desired amount of pork skins on one slice of bread. Top with the other slice of bread. ***Enjoy!*** Tastes like bacon, huh?
Serves: 1

> **DID YOU KNOW?** I arrived at a 5% estimate of prisoners who are wrongly convicted. This was confirmed by an article published in *Playboy* in July 2002, "False Justice," by Chip Rowe. "Five per cent sounds like a reasonable rate of failure of any system – it is a reasonable rate of collateral damage."
> *System Failure* by James F. Love IV

BBQ Beef Sandwich

1 package bbq beef (shredded)	1/2 package lemon drink mix
1-2 teaspoon pickle (chopped)	1 tablespoon salad dressing
1/2 bag bbq chips (crushed)	4 slices bread
1/2 package beef seasoning pack	1-2 packages jalapeno peppers (seeded & diced)
salt & pepper (to taste)	

Mix all ingredients except salad dressing and sliced bread in a large bowl. After it's mixed well, place mixture in a cooking bag and heat in hot pot for 2 hours. When hot, spread salad dressing on bread, add bbq mixture. *Now find a cool drink!*
Serves: 2

DID YOU KNOW? Inmates must walk in a straight line, single-file, and on the right side of the walkway at all times or risk getting a disciplinary case.

Bean and Pork Burritos

1 package chili no beans (heated)	1 package flour tortillas
1/2 bag rice (precooked)	salsa (desired amount)
1 bag refried beans (prepare thick)	2 bags pork skins
1/2 bag jalapeno potato chips (crushed)	2 each jalapenos (seeded and diced)
2 processed meat singles (diced & heated)	

Prepare beans, stir in jalapenos and add cooked rice. Add softened pork skins, use two fingers of hot water to each bag and reseal with a bread-tie to hydrate the pork skins. Add diced meat, crushed jalapeno potato chips, and pouch of chili.

Mix everything together until all ingredients are combined. Spoon out mixture onto a tortilla.

Fold or roll desired way and cook up to an hour. ***Serve pronto!***
Serves: 3

DID YOU KNOW? Inmates are not allowed to talk while in the commissary line.

Feast in a Bag

Bean Burritos

6 each flour tortillas	1/4 bag jalapeno chips (crushed)
1/4 bottle jalapeno cheese	1 tablespoon butter
1/2 bag refried beans	hot water

    Combine beans, butter, jalapeno chips, and a little cheese in a bowl. Add enough water to hydrate beans. Stir well. Make sure bean mixture is moist and thick. Spread remaining jalapeno cheese on tortillas. Spoon bean mixture onto tortillas and roll into a burrito. Cook 45 minutes. Serve with rice.

    Serves: 2

> **DID YOU KNOW?** In the late 1990s, Harris County, Texas, medical examiner Patricia Moore was repeatedly reprimanded by her superiors for pro-prosecution bias. Yet she was still able to keep her position doing official autopsies for the county until 2002. In 2004, a statistical analysis showed Moore diagnosed shaken baby syndrome in infant deaths at a rate several times higher than the national average.
> By Radley Balko (*Reason* magazine), September 15, 2009

Beef Taquitos

1 package beef tips	9 flour tortillas
1/2 cup salsa	1 package chili seasoning
1 package salsa verde chips (crushed)	2 tablespoons jalapeno cheese (optional)

    Shred beef tips and leave moist, removing most of the gravy. In bowl, mix beef tips, salsa, and chili seasoning. Crush chips a little and mix. On tortilla, squirt 1-2 tablespoons of cheese and spread evenly. On edge of tortilla place a spoonful of mixture in a line then roll. Don't tuck the ends. Place in bag and heat for 2 hours.

    Serves: 3

> **DID YOU KNOW?** Most of the items TDCJ buys and sells to the inmates on commissary are made in China: lamps, radios, toiletries, etc.

BEEF TIPS & RICE

1 package beef tips	2 packages beef seasoning
1/4 bag jalapeno chips (crushed)	2 each beef bouillon cubes
1/2 bag rice	2 tablespoons jalapeno cheese
1 tablespoon butter	hot water

For Rice:

Add bouillon cubes, some of the jalapeno chips, some of the cheese, the rice and the butter into your cooking bag. Add about a cup of hot water and stir. Let cook 45 minutes to an hour.

For Beef Tips:

Pour beef tips into cooking bag. Add beef seasoning, the rest of the jalapeno chips, and the rest of the cheese. Stir well and let cook for about an hour.

Pour rice into a bowl and pour beef tips on top. *It's East meets West!*

Serves: 2

DID YOU KNOW? Inmates may be placed in solitary confinement for up to 15 days in a row. But, consecutive terms must be separated by 72 hours.

BEEF VEGETABLE SOUP

2 tablespoons powdered milk	1/2 package cooked rice
1 each tomato juice	1 package beef stew
1-2 tablespoon ketchup	1 package beef seasoning

Heat tomato juice in container. Mix powered milk with 2 tablespoons hot water slowly to avoid lumps and add to tomato juice. Add ketchup and stir. Stir in beef stew. Serve with sandwiches or cheese nips. *Just like mom makes!*

Serves: 2

DID YOU KNOW? Visitors with infants and small children may bring no more than three (3) diapers, baby wipes, and two (2) baby bottles or a "sippy" cup for toddlers into the unit. These items must be stored in a clear plastic bag.

Buttered Noodles

| 1 package chicken seasoning | 3 tablespoons butter |
| 1 sleeve crackers | 1 package noodles |

Cook noodles in water for 10 minutes. Drain all water and add butter and chicken seasoning. Serve with crackers. It's a light and filling lunch.
Serves: 1

> **DID YOU KNOW?** A report by the Correctional Association of New York recommended several policy changes to increase and recognize participation in degree-awarding programs. The report says the principal benefits of college programs in prison are: reduced recidivism because of the enhanced problem-solving skills, greater opportunities for steady employment provided to prisoners, safer and more manageable prison conditions and a cost-effective option for improving public safety.
> Source: *Prison Legal News*, August 2009

Cheeseburger

1 package precooked beef	1 dash chili seasoning packet
1/4 bag jalapeno chips (crushed)	2 tablespoons jalapeno cheese
1 package wheat-n-peanut butter crackers (crushed)	hot water

Put all ingredients into large bowl. Add a little water to moisten. Mixture should be mushy but not too wet. Mix together with your hands (please wash them first) and mold into patties. Put into cooking bag and heat in hot pot.
Serves: 2

> **DID YOU KNOW?** There is no tardiness allowed in prison. Inmates are given disciplinary cases if they turn out late, regardless of who is at fault.

CHEESY POTATO TACOS

1 package beef stew	1/2 bottle jalapeno cheese
1/2 bag powdered milk	1 package flour tortillas
1 bag jalapeno chips (crushed)	hot water

While stirring add powdered milk to hot water slowly to prevent lumps. Add cheese and stir until smooth. Pour crushed chips into bowl and add beef stew and cheese mixture. Stir well. Add desired amount of potato mixture to tortilla and fold into a taco. Cook for an hour or two. *Enjoy!*

Serves: 3

> **DID YOU KNOW?** All visitors arriving at TDCJ must submit to being pat-searched. This includes babies and children and the handicapped (even in wheel-chairs).

CHEESY RICE CASSEROLE

1/2 bag rice	4 tablespoon jalapeno cheese
1/2 bag jalapeno chips (crushed)	hot water
1 package jalapeno (seeded & diced)	

Mix all ingredients with enough water to cover. Cook for at least an hour and serve.

Serves: 3-4

> **DID YOU KNOW?** If an inmate has any physical contact with another inmate they are given a sex case. Yes, this even means a handshake or "an atta girl" (slap on the back). Texas law mandates after a prisoner receives three sex cases, the prisoner must register as a sex offender when released.

Chicken & Cheese Enchiladas

1 each chicken & rice dinner	1/2 bottle salsa
8 flour tortillas	1/4 bottle jalapeno cheese
1/4 bag jalapeno chips (crushed)	2 teaspoons hot water

In a large bowl, add crushed jalapeno chips, 1/2 cheese, and chicken & rice, mix well. Add mixture to each flour tortilla and roll up. Put 4 in each insert. In another large bowl or insert add salsa and remaining cheese with 2 tablespoons of hot water, mix well then pour into inserts with the cheese enchiladas. Cook then eat. ***Yummy!***

Serves: 2

DID YOU KNOW? Prosecutors are increasingly looking on MySpace and other popular social networking sites for information to justify a harsher sentencing for a defendant.
Source: *Prison Legal News*, March 2009

Chicken & Dumplings

1 package chunk chicken (chopped)	1 1/2 packages chicken seasoning
7 tortillas (torn in pieces)	1/2 bag jalapeno chips (crushed)
2 tablespoons jalapeno cheese	4 tablespoons powdered milk
1 package jalapeno pepper (seeded & diced) (desired amount)	hot water

In a bowl, combine seasoning, jalapeno peppers, and chips. Fill insert half full with water and add milk. Slowly add seasoning mixture, cheese, and chicken to insert. Stir well and cook 2 hours. Add slowly tortilla pieces and enough hot water to make creamy. Stir very little and very gently. Cook another 30 minutes.

Serves: 2

DID YOU KNOW? Suicides have now replaced executions as the second leading cause of death on California's death row.
KSBY, 6/12/2007

CHICKEN & RICE

1 bag rice	1 tablespoon jalapeno cheese
1 package chunk chicken	1/4 bag jalapeno chips (crushed)
2 packages chicken seasoning	hot water

Combine all ingredients in rice bag. Add 2-3 cups of hot water. Stir well. Let cook about an hour. Serve with tortilla chips. ***Comforting!***
Serves: 4-6

DID YOU KNOW? When the Bill of Rights was added to the U. S. Constitution, its authors clearly intended to protect the rights of persons accused of crime …Our concern has turned from seeking truth to seeking convictions, and our post-conviction efforts are focused on denying any further review.
Source: www.truthinjustice.org

CHICKEN & RICE SOUP

1 each chicken & rice dinner	water (desired amount)
salt & pepper (desired amount)	cheese (optional)
1 package any seasoning	2 insert cups

Divide chicken & rice between two inserts. Add desired amount of cheese, water, salt & pepper, and packet of seasoning. Mix well and cook at least 40 minutes.
Serves: 2

VARIATION: Replace most of the water with one V8 juice.

DID YOU KNOW? As Justice Brennan stated, "The prisoner's petitions in this nation are the first line of defense for the Constitution of the United States." I have been on the Front Line for 16 years, and I can tell you, from a personal experience and observation, that first line of defense has been breached.
System Failure by James F. Love IV

Feast in a Bag

Chicken & Lemon Pepper Rice

1 bag rice	1 package chunk chicken (chopped)
1-2 each lemon drink mix	1 package chicken seasoning
1 package chili seasoning	hot water
1 package jalapeno pepper (seeded & diced) (desired amount)	1 package pickle (diced) (desired amount)
black pepper to taste	

Combine all ingredients with 2-3 cups hot water and cook 1 and 1/2 hours. Serves: 4

DID YOU KNOW? A sentence of 384,912 years was demanded at the prosecution of Gabriel March Grandos, 22, at Palma de Mallorca, Spain, on March 11, 1972, for failing to deliver 42,768 letters.

Chicken/Bacon Tacos

1 package chunk chicken (chopped)	4 packages cream cheese
1 bag pork skins (crushed)	habenero sauce (desired amount)
1/4 bottle salsa	jalapeno cheese (desired amount)
ranch dressing	water
6 tortillos	

In a large bowl, mix chicken, pork skins, 1/4 bottle salsa, and jalapeno cheese with enough water to make mixture wet and creamy. In a smaller bowl, combine cream cheese and habereno sauce. Spread desired amount of cream cheese/habereno mixture on each tortilla and add chicken mixture. Fold in half and place in doubled chip bag and heat for one hour. Mouth watering! Even better dunked in ranch dressing.

Serves: 6

DID YOU KNOW? Texas inmates are allowed no more than ten (10) names on their approved visitor list.

CHILI CHEESE BURRITOS

6 flour tortillas	1/4 bag refried beans
1/2 bottle jalapeno cheese	1/4 bag jalapeno chips (crushed)
1 package chili with beans	hot water

Open chili bag and add beans and jalapeno chips into the chili package. Add a little hot water to hydrate beans. Stir well. Place chili on tortilla and add 2 tablespoons of cheese to each burrito. Roll into burrito and cook one hour. *Enjoy!*

Serves: 2

DID YOU KNOW? On June 1, 2007, the U.S. Food and Drug Administration issued a warning that toothpaste made in China was found to have diethylene glycol (DEG), a toxic chemical used in anti-freeze and also as a solvent. Over 900,000 tubes have turned up in prisons and hospitals and the toothpaste is still being given to Texas prisoners.
Source: *Prison Legal News*, April 2008

CHILI CHEESE BURRITOS, TWO!

1 package flour tortillas	1/2 package beef seasoning
1/2 package refried beans	1/2 bottle jalapeno cheese
1 package chili with beans	hot water

Prepare beans by adding beef seasoning and hot water. Cook beans and chili separately for an hour. On each flour tortilla, add 1 tablespoon of jalapeno cheese and 1-2 tablespoons of bean and chili mixture. Roll into burritos and put in cooking bag. Cook for 1 hour.

Serves: 3

DID YOU KNOW? All college expenses incurred, while in prison, will either be paid by the inmate at registration or repaid by the inmate upon release. But, if your sentence is over 15 years (within your parole date) the inmate must pay for the tuition prior to attending college.

Chili Cheese Dogs

1 package chicken viennas	1/2 bottle jalapeno cheese
1 package chili no beans	6 slices bread

    Heat chicken viennas in their package and heat chili and jalapeno cheese in a bag. Place chicken viennas on top of bread. Pour chili cheese on top. Serve with chips. ***Messy & fun!***
    Serves: 3

> **DID YOU KNOW?** I arrived at a 5% estimate of prisoners who are wrongly convicted. This was confirmed by an article published in *Playboy* in July 2002, "False Justice," by Chip Rowe. "Five per cent sounds like a reasonable rate of failure of any system – it is a reasonable rate of collateral damage."
> *System Failure* by James F. Love IV

Chili Pie

4 tablespoons jalapeno cheese	1/4 bag corn chips
1 package jalapeno pepper (seeded & diced)	1 package chili (with or without beans)

    Melt cheese with 2 spoonfuls of water in an insert. Place chili package alongside insert and heat at the same time. Put corn chips in a bowl and pour chili over chips. Pour cheese sauce over chili and sprinkle jalapenos over cheese. Just like at the ball park or race track!
    Serves: 2
    VARIATION: Substitute party mix (with the pretzels removed) for the corn chips.

> **DID YOU KNOW?** Lights in the dorm are turned on every morning at 3:30 a.m. Breakfast starts at 4:00 a.m.; lunch at 10:30 a.m.; and dinner at 4:00 p.m. Lights go out at 10:30 p.m.

CHIMICHANGAS

1 package tuna	1 package flour tortillas
1 package chicken seasoning	1/2 bottle jalapeno cheese
1 package chili seasoning	1/2 bag jalapeno chips (crushed)
1/4 bag pork skins	1 package jalapeno pepper (seeded & diced)
1/4 package pickle (chopped)	

Mix tuna, chicken seasoning, chili seasoning, jalapeno pepper, and pickle together then add pork skins and jalapeno chips. Align 5 flour tortillas so they overlap at ends. Add a small amount of mixture along the width of the tortilla, roll up like a burrito, and put in a bag. Put as much cheese as you need to cover the chimichanga and cook at least 1 hour. Try serving with sala verde chips.

Serves: 2

DID YOU KNOW? TDCJ prisoners are only given 2 apples and 2 oranges a year; one of each at Thanksgiving and Christmas.

CHOPA'S

1 package chili or beef seasoning	1/2 bottle jalapeno cheese
1 package jalapeno peppers (seeded & diced)	1/2 bag corn chips (crushed into fine powder)
1 package summer sausage or other meat (cut-up)	hot water

Mix chips, seasoning packet, cheese, and water into "dough." Spread flat into hand size portions. Drop 2 or 3 spoonfuls of the meat, jalapeno and 2 tablespoons of cheese onto middle. Fold over and seal together. Cook in chip bag to preserve shape. Make sure bag has no holes – double bag if necessary. ***Authentic!***

Serve: 3

DID YOU KNOW? Inmates and their living areas may be searched (and/or destroyed) at any time by staff.

Feast in a Bag

CHORIZO TACOS

1 package flour tortillas	1 tablespoon jalapeno cheese
1 package chili with beans	1/2 bag bbq chips (crushed)
1 package chicken viennas (diced then smashed to a paste)	

Combine the mashed chicken viennas with the chili. Add bbq chips and mix well. Add jalapeno cheese and mix well. Cook 4-5 hours. Add meat mixture to tortillas and fold into tacos, cook 1 hour. ***South of the border!***

Serves: 3

> **DID YOU KNOW?** Inmates are not allowed to correspond with other inmates unless they are immediate family members. But, they may correspond with a co-defendant if approved by the warden.

COUNTRY RICE

1 bag rice (pre-cooked)	1 package beef seasoning
1 package chili seasoning	pepper to taste
1/2 cup jalapeno chips (crushed)	1/2 cup pork skins (crushed)
1 package processed meat slices (chopped)	1 package pickle (diced)(desired amount)
1 tablespoon jalapeno cheese	

Mix all ingredients in a large bowl. Put into cooking bag or bowl with lid. Pour very hot water over mixture to cover everything well and let sit for 5 minutes or until rice is done.

Serves: 2

> **DID YOU KNOW?** A writ of habeas corpus is an order directing a person who has custody of another to show cause why they are holding them. Thus, the actual writ itself is nothing more than a summons.
> *Understanding Habeas Corpus* by Walter M. Reaves, Jr. Attorney at Law

DELIGHTFUL TUNA NACHOS

1 package tuna	1 package chicken seasoning
1 package chili with beans	tortilla chips
2 tablespoons powdered milk	1 tablespoon salsa
2 tablespoons salad dressing	1 tablespoon jalapeno cheese
3 teaspoons jalapeno hot sauce	3 tablespoons hot water (in plastic insert)

In plastic insert, combine chicken seasoning mix and dry milk. Add water slowly to avoid lumps. Mix until smooth. Add remaining ingredients and stir well. Place package of chili with beans alongside insert and cook both for 1 1/2 hours. Pour chili with beans over tortilla chips. Follow with tuna mixture. Top with salsa. Add more jalapeno hot sauce if desired.

Serves: 2 (large)

VARIATION: Substitute crushed salsa verde chips and crushed jalapeno chips for the chicken seasoning mix.

DID YOU KNOW? More than 40 percent of Iowa's prison population is classified as having "special needs," with either behavioral or mental health problems. Radio Iowa, June 4, 2007

DELUXE MEXICAN NACHOS

1 package crumbled beef patty	1/4 bottle jalapeno cheese
tortilla chips	1/4 bag jalapeno chips (crushed)
2 packages jalapeno peppers (seeded & diced)	

Mix crumbled beef patty, a little jalapeno cheese, and jalapeno chips; cook one hour. Pour beef mixture over tortilla chips and top with cheese, salsa, and jalapeno peppers. *A Mexican fiesta!*

Serves: 2

DID YOU KNOW? No hair brushes are sold to the female inmates on commissary.

DELIGHTFUL TUNA NACHOS, TWO!

1 package tuna	tortilla chips
1/2 bottle jalapeno cheese	1/2 bag powdered milk
1/8 bag jalapeno chips (crushed)	hot water
1 package jalapeno (seeded & diced)	1 package ranch dressing

In your cooking jar or insert, add powdered milk. Add a little hot water slowly to avoid lumps. Add jalapeno cheese and ranch dressing and stir. Add more water if needed. Add jalapeno, tuna, and jalapeno chips. Stir well. Let cook about an hour. Pour over tortillas chips and top with jalapenos. Serve with salsa. *Finger licking good!*

Serves: 2

VARIATION: To spice things up a bit, try combining salsa verde chips and nacho chips with the plain tortilla chips in equal parts. The dish will be colorful as well as tasty!

> **DID YOU KNOW?** Since 1980, the number of female prisoners have risen 762 percent.

ENCHILADAS

1 bag corn chips (crushed)	1 package precooked beef
1 package chili seasoning	2 bags hot fries (crushed)
1/2 bottle jalapeno cheese	hot water
1 each tomato juice (regular) (can or bottle)	strips of paper (at least 3"x 4" or bigger)

In a bowl, pour crushed corn chips and chili seasoning, and mix well. Pour water and mix well until you have a moist but firm mixture. Spoon mixture onto strips of paper, mash flat. Spoon precooked beef and some cheese on top, and roll into the shape of an enchilada. Let cook 1 hour. Mix crushed hot fries and tomato juice and heat. Heat remaining cheese separately; pour tomato juice/hot fries sauce over enchiladas and top with cheese. Serve with rice and beans. *Spicy!*

Serves: 4-5

ENTICING ENCHILADAS

1 package chili no beans	1 package chili with beans
3 flour tortillas	1 package chili seasoning
1 package beef tips	1 bottle jalapeno cheese
1 package processed meat singles (chopped)	1 package summer sausage (chopped)
1 bottle salsa	

Combine all meats in a big bowl. Add seasoning, both chili's, 1/2 bottle salsa and mix well. Spread cheese and mixture over three tortillas. Fold the tortillas in half and place in a bag or pickle bag. Mix and cook separately leftover mixture, 1/2 bottle salsa, cheese and a little water to use as a topping. Cook for 2 or 3 hours.

Serves: 4

DID YOU KNOW? The Dutch Ministry of Justice recently purchased 40,000 rolls of specialty toilet paper printed with recommendations for good hygiene, safe sex, and coping with aggression.
Prison Legal News, August 2009

GUMBO

1 package beef stew	1 package summer sausage (diced)
1 tablespoon jalapeno squeeze cheese (or more if desired)	1 each tomato juice (spicy, low sodium, or regular) (can or bottle)
1/2 bag jalapeno chips (crushed)	1 package processed meat single

Combine all ingredients and cook 4-5 hours and pour over buttered rice. ***Delicious!***

Serves: 2

DID YOU KNOW? Texas inmates are allowed eye exams every 2 years. If they have no one to send in a pair of plastic glasses from the free-world then they are issued a TDCJ pair. These are black, thick, ugly frames that resemble "Buddy Holly" glasses. Inmates refer to these glasses as B.C.'s (Birth Control) or R.P.G.'s (Rape Prevention Goggles).

FAST & DELICIOUS BURRITO

1/2 cup refried beans	1 package flour tortillas
1/2 bottle jalapeno cheese	1/4 bag salsa verde chips (crushed)
1 package jalapeno pepper (chopped)	1 package chili (with or without beans)
	hot water

In a plastic cup, mix refried beans with just enough hot water to come to top of beans; let set until partially hydrated.

Open pouch of chili and add crushed chips and chopped jalapeno pepper directly into pouch.

Spoon refried beans on flour tortilla and spoon 2 or 3 spoonfuls chili mixture on top of refried beans.

Squeeze a line of cheese across tortilla mixture and roll up into a burrito. Place burrito, loose end down, in empty chip bag or insert cup for hot pot. Make 3 more burritos and add to the one. Heat bag of burritos 30-40 minutes.

Serves: 3

VARIATIONS:

Add salsa inside or outside of burrito when done.

Add cheese on top of burrito when done.

Add jalapeno and salad dressing mixture on top of burritos when done.

Add precooked beef or beef tips to chili mixture.

Add crushed salsa verde chips mixed with salad dressing as a topping for cooked burrito

---

DID YOU KNOW? As stated by Senior District Court Judge Chares E. Wyzanski, Jr., (sitting by designation), in *U.S. v. Twomey*, 510 F.2d 634, 640 (7th Cir. 1975): "While a criminal trial is not a game in which the participants are expected to enter the ring with a near match in skills, neither is it a sacrifice of unarmed prisoners to gladiators."

System Failure by James F. Love IV

☺ **HELPFUL HINT!!** Pickle bags or cereal bags make the best cooking bags because they are harder to puncture than chip bags.

FISH STIX

2 packages tuna	1 tablespoon jalapeno cheese
1 bag salsa verde chips	1 package chili seasoning
1 bag corn chips (crushed)	typing paper (tear in fourths)
1 tablespoon salad dressing	hot water
salsa (desired amount)	1 package instant potatoes (desired flavor)
1/2 bag jalapeno chips (crushed)	
1-2 packages jalapeno peppers (seeded & diced)	1-2 packages chicken seasoning

Breading: Crush bag of corn chips (make small hole at top of bag to let air out; place chips in between a towel and walk on bag until chips are crushed. It takes 30 seconds. Place crushed chips in tortilla chip bag, add 1/2 cup – 3/4 cup of water, 1/2 bag of salsa verde chips, one chili seasoning packet, salsa (couple of squirts), and cheese (one squirt with top off). Mash around in bag until well mixed. (You may add more water for desired wetness of crust.)

Fish Mixture: In large bowl, mix 2 packets of tuna, minced jalapeno pepper, 1/2 bag jalapeno chips, 1/2 salsa verde chips, chicken seasoning packets, salsa, cheese, instant potatoes, salad dressing and enough water to make a creamy paste.

Fish Stix: On square of paper, spread 1 spoon of breading mixture and flatten it to cover the square. Place 1/2 spoonful of tuna mixture on top of breading and roll into stick. Place in bag.

Double bag and cook for at least 2 hours.

Serves: 4

VARIATION: Add teaspoon of coffee to fish mixture. To decrease fish taste and give an oriental flavor.

DID YOU KNOW? Inmates must write their names and TDCJ number on every envelope & piece of paper (or they are given a disciplinary case). Inmates are allowed to have pre-printed envelopes sent in, but they are not allowed to have pre-printed paper.

☺ **HELPFUL HINT!** Dairy products help ease the burn of hot foods.

Feast in a Bag

Hash Browns

5 bags hot fries (crushed)	1 tablespoon beans
1 package ham (chopped fine)	hot water

Combine ingredients and add a few tablespoons of hot water and stir. Consistency should be moist but not too mushy. Spread evenly in bowl and top with ketchup or cheese.

Serves: 1

> **DID YOU KNOW?** Florists in Colorado are crying out against a prison program that is competing against them, undercutting their prices due to the help of prisoner slave labor.
> *Prison Legal News*, August 2009

Holiday Fruit Salad

2 each oranges	3 tablespoons orange juice
1 bag fruit & nut mix	2 each apples (cored and thinly sliced)

Peel and section oranges. Combine with thinly sliced apples, fruit & nut mix, and orange juice. ***Fruity!***

Serves: 2

> **DID YOU KNOW?** Research compiled by Gregory A. Hubner of Yale University and Sanford C. Gordon of New York University revealed that trial judges hand out more prison and jail time to defendants just before they come up for reelection. Once the numbers were crunched results revealed that just before election time judges sentenced defendants from 12 to 16 months longer. No judge included in the study handed down more lenient sentences. Pennsylvania judges close to reelection sentenced defendants to "more than two thousand years of additional incarceration" during that 9-year period.
> *Prison Legal News*, April 2009

Hot Ham & Cheese Sandwich

4 slices bread	1 tablespoon jalapeno cheese
1/8 package pickle (diced)	1 package processed meat singles (diced)
1/4 bag jalapeno chips (crushed)	

Combine the meat, cheese, jalapeno chips, and pickle into your cooking bag. Let cook 30 minutes. Spoon mixture onto bread, top with additional slice of bread to create sandwiches. Serve with chips. *Tasty!*

Serves: 1-2

DID YOU KNOW? Richard Honeck was sentenced to life imprisonment in the U.S. in 1899, after having murdered his former schoolteacher. He was released on parole on December 20, 1963, at the age of 84. He spent 64 years in prison only receiving one letter (a 4-line note from his brother in 1904) and 2 visitors, a friend in 1904 and a newspaper reporter in 1963.

Hot Tuna Casserole

1 package tuna	1/3 bag rice
2 tablespoons jalapeno cheese	1/2 package chicken seasoning
2 tablespoons picante sauce or salsa	1 package jalapeno or pickle (diced)

Mix all ingredients with enough water to cover. Cook and serve.
Serves: 2

DID YOU KNOW? U.S. District Court Judge Samuel B. Kent of Texas pleaded guilty to lying to federal investigators and admitted that he had engaged in nonconsensual sexual conduct. He received a 33 month prison sentence on May 11, 2000, and was also ordered to pay restitution to his victims.
Source: *Prison Legal News*, August 2009

HOT WINGLESS WRAPS

2 packages chunk chicken	1 bottle hot sauce
8-10 tortillas	5 packages cream cheese
1/2 bag jalapeno chips or bbq chips (crushed)	1 package ranch dressing

In a large bowl, mix chicken with bottle of hot sauce. Let marinade for 3 hours. Mix in 1/2 bag chips. Spread desired amount of cream cheese on tortilla. Then spoon chicken mixture on top of the cheese and roll. Place in a doubled chip bag and cook for one hour. Serve with ranch dressing for a zesty bite.

Serves: 3

DID YOU KNOW? Much of the conflict surrounding writs can be attributed to evolving views of the underlying theory behind habeas corpus. Generally, three "models" of review have been developed: the "constitutional model," the "process model," and the "innocence model." *Understanding Habeas Corpus* by Walter M. Reaves, Jr. Attorney at Law

INDIAN RICE

1 bag rice	1/2 bag hot peanuts
1 package chicken vienna	1/4 package pickle (diced)
1/2 bag jalapeno chips (crushed)	1 each tomato juice (can or bottle)
1 package chicken seasoning	2 tablespoons salsa
1 package jalapeno peppers (seeded & diced)	hot water

Combine all ingredients and put in a cooking bag. Stir well and let heat for at least one hour. Serve with tortilla chips. ***Middle Eastern!***

Serves: 4-6

DID YOU KNOW? Inmates are allowed to shower every day for about 10 minutes. When the unit is on lockdown, inmates are allowed one shower every third day for about 5 minutes.

JALAPENO POPPERS

5 bags hot fries	1 package refried beans
1/2 bag cheese puffs	chicken seasoning (desired amount)
10 package jalapeno peppers	typing paper (tear in fourths)
1/2 bag jalapeno chips	hot water
1/2 bottle jalapeno cheese	

Crust: Crush hot fries, cheese puffs, and jalapeno chips as fine as possible and combine. Add enough water to make thick paste. Spread out a thin layer on a square piece of paper.

Bean mixture: Make refried beans with a lot of cheese and chicken seasoning (desired amount).

Poppers: Clean and remove seeds from peppers. Cut in half. Place a spoon of bean mixture on layer of crust then the jalapeno half. Roll up the popper.

Double bag and cook for two hours.

Serves: 4

DID YOU KNOW? The housing areas do not have refrigerators or microwaves. Sodas must be drank at room temperature.

MACKEREL/SARDINES IN RICE

1/2 bag rice	2 tablespoons salad dressing
1/2 package seasoning of choice	1 package jalapeno pepper (seeded & diced)
1 package mackerel or smoked sardines	

Directions: In a cooking bag, precook rice and add mackerel or smoked sardines, jalapeno pepper, 1/2 seasoning packet, salad dressing. Mix well. Cook one hour. Serve with tortilla chips or crackers.

Serves: 2

DID YOU KNOW? Each inmate is allowed to have up to two (2) visitors per visit, for two hours each week on either Saturday or Sunday.

MACKEREL WITH NO COOK TOMATO SAUCE

3 dashes chicken seasoning	3 each garlic pills (oil only)
salsa (desired amount)	1 package mackerel (well rinsed & drained)
salt & pepper (to taste)	

In a small bowl, mix salsa, salt, pepper, garlic, and chicken seasoning. Spoon over mackerel and serve with tortilla chips.

Serves: 1

> **DID YOU KNOW?** Chief Judge Learned Hand, who had opined in reference to granting absolute immunity to prosecutors, "It has been thought in the end better ... to leave unredressed the wrongs done by dishonest officers than to subject those who try to do their duty to the constant dread of retaliation."
> Source: *Prison Legal News*, March 2009

MEATY NACHOS

1 package processed meat singles	jalapeno cheese (desired amount)
1 package precooked beef (well rinsed & drained)	salsa (if desired)
	water

In precooked beef pouch, combine chopped processed meat single, water, and jalapeno cheese. Heat for an hour. Pour over desired chips and drizzle with jalapeno cheese. ***Mouth watering!***

Serves: 2

> **DID YOU KNOW?** After weeks of pressure, Harris County District Attorney Charles Rosenthal resigned Friday (2-15-08) amid a scandal involving romantic, pornographic, and racial e-mails found on his county computer.
> Source: KPRC Local 2 News

MENUDO

1 bag pork skins	1 package chili seasoning
1/4 bag jalapeno chips (crushed)	hot water
1 package jalapeno (seeded & diced)	

Combine above ingredients in your cooking bag. Fill 3/4 of the bag with hot water. Stir well and let cook for 45 minutes. Serve with tortillas or tortilla chips. *Zesty!*

Serves: 2

DID YOU KNOW? On unit lockdown, inmates are given a brown bag sack meal three times a day that consists of one peanut butter and jelly sandwich and one meat product.

MEXICAN PIZZA

3 each matzo crackers	1 package precooked beef
1/2 package refried beans	1/4 bottle jalapeno cheese
1/4 package powdered milk	4 packages cream cheese
1/2 bottle salsa	1 package chili seasoning
3 packages jalapeno peppers (seeded & diced)	hot water

Cook precooked beef and season to taste. Cook refried beans and season to taste. In an insert fill half way with powdered milk and then 1/4 of jalapeno cheese. Add hot water slowly to avoid lumps and make a thick creamy cheese sauce. Take matzo crackers and layer meat, beans, cheese sauce, salsa, cream cheese, peppers. Then sprinkle chili seasoning on top.

Serves: 3

DID YOU KNOW? Trusty status inmates receive four or five contact visits a month with every visitor (friend or family). All other general population inmates receive three contact visits with an immediate family member a month.

Feast in a Bag

MEXICAN RICE

1 bag rice	1 each tomato juice
1/2 bag pork skins (crushed)	1/2 bag jalapeno chips (crushed)
1 package chicken, beef or chili seasoning	1 package summer sausage or other meat (chopped)
1/2 cup hot water	

Combine all ingredients in a bowl and mix. Place in hot pot and cook 1 hour. Serve with nacho chips or salsa verde chips.

Serves: 4

> **DID YOU KNOW?** Nationally, 7.3 million children have at least one parent in jail or prison.

MORE THAN CHEESE QUESADILLAS

2 packages jalapeno peppers (seeded & cut into slivers)	1 package instant potatoes (herb or butter flavored)
1 package flour tortillas	1 bottle jalapeno cheese
1 package pre-cooked crumbled beef patty (rinse well)	1 package summer sausage (cut into 1/4 inch circles)
salsa	1 each large cooking bag

Cut all tortillas into quarters while cooking mashed potatoes according to package directions. Set all ingredients in an assembly line. Take one flour tortilla quarter and spread mashed potatoes on top (about 1/2 spoonful). Then place summer sausage, beef patty crumbles, squirt jalapeno cheese, and salsa on top of mashed potatoes. Place another flour tortilla on top of this to seal together. Place in bag. Repeat ingredient in order 19 more times filling up your cooking bag. Cook in hot pot for 1 hour.

Serves: 5

SUGGESTION: Serve with rice & beans for a complete meal.

> **DID YOU KNOW?** Inmates are not allowed to have playing cards or dice for fear of gambling. But, they are allowed to have dominos.

Nachos Deluxe

1 bag tortilla chips	1/2 cup refried beans
2 tablespoon salad dressing	1/2 cup salsa
1 package precooked beef or beef tips	1/2 cup salsa verde chips (crushed)
1 bottle jalapeno cheese	hot water
2 package jalapeno peppers (seeded & diced)	1 package chili (with or without beans)

Line bowl standing tortilla chips up, then keep going with chips standing, leaving a hole in the center of the bowl.

Put refried beans in cup, add water to top off beans, and let set until beans are hydrated.

Heat precooked beef and chili about 30-40 minutes.

While chili and meat are heating, mix salad dressing and crushed salsa verde chips. Set aside.

Pour refried beans in center hole in bowl. Squeeze some cheese on top. Cover with precooked beef. Pour chili over meat. Squeeze cheese on top of chili, squeeze cheese around on chips.

Pour salsa on cheese. Dollop salad dressing and chip mixture on top. Sprinkle chopped jalapeno pepper on top as a finishing touch.

Eat and enjoy, using chips to dip from the center of the bowl, done this way the chips don't get soggy. ***Yum!***

Serves: 4

DID YOU KNOW? If a jury finds someone guilty, and there is compelling evidence the person is innocent, judges have the power to overturn the jury's conviction (that doesn't happen a lot in the real world). Giving jurors more power to acquit is based on the constitutional principle that it's better to let guilty people go free than to allow the innocent to be punished.
Source: *Prison Legal News*, June 2009

☺ **HELPFUL HINT!** Always double your cooking bags to ensure water doesn't get inside and drown your meal.

Feast in a Bag

ORIENTAL RICE

1 each orange/pineapple juice	1 each peach drink mix
1 bag rice	1 package chili seasoning
1/4 cup jalapeno chips (crushed)	sunflower seeds or nuts
1 package pickle (chopped) (desired amount)	1 package tuna or processed meat slices (chopped)
1 package chicken seasoning	

Cook rice with chili seasoning until done. Add peach drink mix, desired amount of seeds or nuts, and tuna or meat. Cook for 1 hour. Put chicken seasoning on top.

Serves: 4

> **DID YOU KNOW?** Garcia, 38, is among thousands of prisoners at more than 20 federal facilities in the U.S. where inmates now have email inboxes. By the spring of 2011, all 114 federal prisons are expected to have email available for inmates.

PASTA PARMESAN

2 packages chicken soup	cheese puffs (handful) (crushed)
1 package summer sausage (cut up)	water (desired amount)

In a large cooking bag, cook soups in just enough water to cover noodles (leave noodles fairly long) with summer sausage for about 10 minutes. Once fully cooked pour into large white bowl and mix with one chicken seasoning packet. Top with finely crushed cheese puffs. Tastes just like parmesan cheese.

Serves: 2

> **DID YOU KNOW?** Thomas Starkie's Evidence 751 (1824) - Under that standard, less than a 99% probability of a defendant's guilt constitutes reasonable doubt, and he or she must be acquitted.
> *Kirstin Blaise Lobato's Unreasonable Conviction* by Hans Sherrer

PASTA SALAD

1 package chili soup	1 package turkey or chicken meat
chips, pretzels, or party mix (crushed)	1 package pickle (cut into 1/4 inch chunks)
1 package trail mix (may substitute with peanuts or other nuts)	1 tablespoon salad dressing or sandwich spread
1/2 package sweetener	

Cook soup without flavor packet. Rinse and drain noodles. Mix the following together – 1/2 flavor packet, salad dressing, pickle, and sweetener. Mix into noodles. Add meat and trail mix (take out any banana chips) and pour over noodles. Mix well and serve. ***Dig in!***

Serves: 2

DID YOU KNOW? All hygiene items used by the inmates must be purchased at the unit commissary. The state of Texas does not supply deodorant or shampoo to the inmates.

PASTA SALAD, TWO!

2 tablespoon salad dressing	1 each lemon drink mix
1/4 package pickle (diced)	1 package trail mix (raisins only)
1 tablespoon sunflower seeds	salt & pepper (to taste)
1 each soup (cooked with seasoning and drained)	1 package jalapeno pepper (seeded & diced)

Cook soup with flavor packet. Drain noodles. Combine all ingredients in bowl and mix well. Add desired amount of salt and pepper. Serve with crackers of your choice.

Serves: 2

DID YOU KNOW? The longest recorded prison sentences were ones of **7,109 years,** awarded to 2 confidence tricksters in Iran (formerly Persia) on June 15, 1969.

PAZONES

1/2 bottle jalapeno cheese	1 bag hot fries (crushed)
1 package flour tortillas	1/2 bottle salsa
2 packages jalapeno peppers (seeded & diced)	2 packages chicken vienna (chopped small) (can substitute either meats or summer sausage)
2 packages processed meat singles (chopped small)	

Mix peppers, meats and hot fries together until well blended. Take four tortillas and spread one side with cheese. Add meat mixture and top with one or two teaspoons of salsa. Fold in half. Place 3 in a chip bag and cook for at least 1 hour in hot-pot.

Serves: 3

DID YOU KNOW? Disciplinary decisions may be appealed by filing a grievance. Most appeals are not decided until after the inmate has served their disciplinary punishment sentence. Most appeals are lost.

PEANUT RICE

1 package rice	1 each beef bouillon cube
1 each cranberry juice	1 package salted peanuts (spicy)

Open package of rice and add crushed beef bouillon cube and peanuts and mix well with a spoon. Add enough cranberry juice to cover the rice mixture with about 3/4" of juice over the top of the rice. Place in hot pot and cook until done.

Serves: 2

DID YOU KNOW? Juan Corona, a Mexican-American was sentenced to 25 consecutive life terms for murdering 25 migrant farm workers he had hired, killed, and buried in 1970-1971 near Feather River, Yuba City, California, on February 5, 1973 at Fairfield, California.

Pizza Fold

1 bottle jalapeno cheese	1 jar habenero sauce
1 package chili seasoning	4 flour tortillas
1 package ranch dressing	1 bag jalapeno chips (crushed)
1 package jalapeno peppers (seeded) & diced) (desired amount)	1 package summer sausage (sliced thin)

On tortillas, spread salad dressing, cheese, sliced sausage, and sprinkle some seasoning on top. Add some crushed chips, chopped jalapenos, ranch dressing and fold over. Cook in a hot pot about 2 hours.

Serves: 4

> **DID YOU KNOW?** Too often, law enforcement uses the press as a prosecutorial tool. Good reporters are taught to be skeptical. The problem with judge-and-jury commentators is that they aren't trained as journalists at all.
> Source: *Reader's Digest* by Michael Crowley

Po' Man's Burrito

1 package flour tortillas	1 package beef seasoning
1 package refried beans	1 bottle jalapeno cheese
hot water	

Cook beans with beef seasoning then spread mixture on flour tortilla and apply cheese. Fold into tacos or roll into burritos and insert into a cooking bag. Cook for 1 hour.

Serves: 3

> **DID YOU KNOW?** It costs roughly $29,000 to house a single inmate for a year.
> Source: *The Week*, September 25, 2009

POTATO SOUP

1/4 bag jalapeno chips (crushed)	4 tablespoons jalapeno cheese
1 sleeve saltine crackers	1 tablespoon butter
1 package instant potato (any flavor)	hot water

Equally divide ingredients and place into two (2) inserts. Add water one inch from the top of insert and cook for one hour. After one hour stir mixture and empty into large bowl. Add hot water if not soupy enough. Garnish with saltine crackers.

Serves: 2

> **DID YOU KNOW?** As soon as inmates reach the entrance to the chow hall they are given 20 minutes to eat meals in the chow hall. By the time they reach the table and sit down to eat, it leaves less then 10 minutes to consume their food. So, if your food is too hot or frozen, you leave HUNGRY!

POTLUCK SOUP

1/4 bag jalapeno chips (crushed)	1/4 package pickle (diced)
1/4 bag pork skins (crushed)	2 tablespoons jalapeno cheese
1 package chili soup (crush the noodles)	4-5 dashes habanero hot sauce
	hot water

In cooking jar or insert, combine above ingredients including chili seasoning packet from the soup. Let cook 15 minutes. Serve with tortilla chips. ***Enjoy!***

Serves: 1

> **DID YOU KNOW?** Inmates that are in solitary confinement are allowed out of their cell only one (1) time each day to shower. The guard picks the time of the shower, not the inmate. The inmates are escorted to the shower with their hands cuffed behind their backs. While the inmate is in the shower, the guard searches the inmate's cell.

Punk Rock Tacos

6 flour tortillas	1/4 bag dried beans
6 tablespoons jalapeno cheese	3 packages ranch dressing
1/2 bag jalapeno chips (crushed fine)	seasoning (desired amount)
1 package summer sausage or processed meat slices (cubed)	

Prepare beans and season to taste and set aside. Place cubed summer sausage or processed meat slices and crushed chips in separate bowls and heat cheese in an insert. On each tortilla spread a layer of beans, followed by a layer of cheese. Top with some meat and a layer of chips. Then squeeze 1/2 packet of ranch dressing before folding the tortilla in half to make a taco. Place 3 tacos in each cooking bag and cook in hot pot for 1 hour.

Serves: 2

DID YOU KNOW? The hot pots that cook prisoner's food never reach the boiling point.

Red Beans and Rice

2 packages chili with beans (rinsed)	1/4 bag jalapeno chips (crushed)
3/4 bag rice (cooked)	hot sauce (desired amount)
salt & pepper (optional)	hot water
1 package processed meat singles (chopped)	chicken seasoning (desired amount)

In a large bag cook rinsed chili with beans, processed ham, jalapeno chips, chicken seasoning, water, salt & pepper, and hot sauce. Once cooked, pour over bed of cooked and buttered rice.

Serves: 4

DID YOU KNOW? The Parties to a Crime Law in Texas has allowed the perpetrator of the crime to accuse another person (often innocent) of committing the crime, and then the perpetrator plea bargains for a lesser sentence while the person he/she accuses has a much longer sentence.

Feast in a Bag

SARDINE DIP

1 package sardines (any flavor)	jalapeno chips (handful) (crushed)
1/2 cup rice (precooked)	jalapeno cheese (optional)
salad dressing (desired amount)	

Mix together in large bowl precooked rice, sardines, crushed jalapeno chips, salad dressing, and jalapeno cheese. Eat with either crackers or chips. Serve with jalapenos on the side. ***Munchy and satisfying!***

Serves: 2

> **DID YOU KNOW?** 2.3 million Americans are in prison, while another 5.1 million are on probation or parole. With only 5 percent of the world's population, the U.S. has 25 percent of the world's prisoners in its jails.
> Source: *The Week*, September 25, 2009

SARDINES & RICE

1 package sardines (in hot sauce)	1 package chili seasoning
1/2 bag rice	1 package chicken seasoning
1/4 bag jalapeno chips (crushed)	hot water

Remove spines from the sardines. In a bowl, combine sardines, chili seasoning, chicken seasoning, jalapeno chips, and rice. Add enough hot water to hydrate the rice. Stir well and transfer to a cooking bag. Pour the hot water into the bowl you just took the mixture from. Stir to pick up left over seasonings. Pour water into the cooking bag and stir well. Add more water if needed. Cook for 1 hour and serve with tortilla chips.

Serves: 2

> **DID YOU KNOW?** There are more than 10.65 million people in prisons worldwide. That figure includes 850,000 in "administrative detention" in China. Almost half of all prisoners are held in only three countries: Russia, China and the United States.
> *Prison Legal News*, April 2010

SAUSAGE BURRITOS

1 package rice	1 package flour tortillas
1 package chili seasoning	1 package chili with beans
1/2 bottle jalapeno cheese	1/4 bottle salsa
1 package summer sausage (cut-up)	hot water

Mix chili seasoning with the rice and cook until done. Add summer sausage and chili and stir well. Spoon into a flour tortilla and squeeze jalapeno cheese on top then layer with salsa. Roll-up and place 3 – 4 burritos in chip bags and cook in hot-pot for at least an hour.

Serves: 3

> **DID YOU KNOW?** Volunteer groups come to the prisons to sing, preach, teach, and to provide other help.

SCALLOPED POTATOES

1 bag jalapeno chips (leave whole)	1 package beef stew
1/2 cup powdered milk	1-1/2 cup water
1/2 bottle jalapeno cheese	

In large bowl mix water and powdered milk until smooth. Add cheese and mix well. Then add the pot roast and mix. In two plastic inserts, layer jalapeno chips and cheese sauce, alternating until about 1 inch below top of insert. Top layer should be the sauce mix. Cook in hot-pot at least 1 hour, stirring occasionally. Add water if needed.

Serves: 2

> **DID YOU KNOW?** On May 12, 2007, Mary Cristan, 44, was pronounced dead at 11:58 p.m. She was found lying in her cell with her hands bound at the TDCJ Hobby Unit. They are looking at her 26 year old cellmate as a possible suspect, because she (the cellmate) had scratches and abrasions. Cristan was scheduled for release less than 2 months later, in July 2007.
> Source: *Waco Tribune-Herald*, May 15, 2007

Feast in a Bag

SHISH KABOBS WITH RICE

1 package chicken seasoning	2 packages processed meat singles
1 package pickle (chopped small)	1 bag rice (precooked)
1 package beef seasoning	juice from 2 jalapeno peppers
1/2 bag jalapeno chips (crushed)	popcicle sticks (3-4 per person)
1 package jalapeno pepper (seeded & diced)	2 packages summer sausage (sliced thin)

Shish kabobs: Slice summer sausage into thin slices widthwise. Slice processed meat singles into about 4x4 sections. Cut pickles and jalapeno peppers into small size pieces – big enough to slide onto sticks. Alternately slide each of these onto sticks.

Rice: In a large bowl mix precooked rice, jalapeno chips, chicken and beef seasoning, and juice from 2 jalapeno peppers. Divide rice mixture into four bags. Place four (4) kabobs in the bed of rice and cook for 2 hours. ***Tastefully appetizing!***

Serves: 4

DID YOU KNOW? For a female inmate, getting a haircut is a privilege. They have to stay free of a disciplinary case for 90 days to have their hair cut.

"SKIN OF THE PIG" BURRITO

1 package flour tortillas	1 bag pork skins (broken up)
1 package chili seasoning	hot water
1 package jalapeno pepper (seeded & diced)	

In bowl, combine pork skins, chili seasoning, desired amount of cheese, diced jalapenos, and enough hot water to fully saturate pork skins. Stir well. Spread desired amount of cheese on tortilla and add pork skin mixture. Fold into a taco and cook for 1 hour.

Serves: 3

DID YOU KNOW? The inmate's tooth brush is only about 2 inches long from the handle to the end with bristles.

SOUTHWESTERN STYLE CHICKEN QUESADILLAS

1 package flour tortillas	butter (desired amount)
jalapeno cheese (desired amount)	salsa (desired amount)
2 packages chili with beans (well rinsed)	2 packages chunk chicken (chopped)

Chop chicken into small pieces and mix in large bowl with well rinsed chili with beans. Place a spoonful of mixture on buttered tortilla. Squirt a generous amount of cheese and salsa on the top of the chicken mixture. Fold the tortilla in half. Cook for at least an hour. *Cheesy and satisfying!*

Serves: 3

DID YOU KNOW? A Taiwanese man received 5 months in jail for removing the toupee from a legislator's head. The victim felt the wig made him look prettier and the judge felt that removing it took away the freedom to wear what he wanted.
Source: *Details*, October 2009

SPICY POTATO BURRITO

1 package flour tortillas	1 package chili with beans
1/2 package refried beans	1/2 package pickle (diced)
1/2 bottle jalapeno cheese	1 package jalapeno chips (crushed)
1 package jalapeno peppers (seeded and diced)	

In a cooking bag combine chips, chili with beans, refried beans, diced pickle and diced jalapeno pepper. Cook in hot pot for 30 minutes to warm.

Take a flour tortilla and spread jalapeno cheese evenly and then apply mixture. Fold into tacos and put into cooking bag. Cook for 1-2 hours.

Serves: 3

DID YOU KNOW? The inmates that work in the Administration (Wardens) or Command (Ranks) buildings are given "special" clothes to wear. The rest of the inmate population has to wear heavily stained clothes, even if they also work with free-world bosses.

SPICY GUMBO

1 package beef seasoning	1 package beef stew
1 package mackerel	1 package chunk chicken
1 bag rice (precooked)	1/2 to 1 package chili seasoning
1 bag jalapeno chips (crushed)	1 bag pork skins (crushed)
1 package chicken seasoning	hot water
1 package jalapeno peppers (seeded and diced) (desired amount)	1 package summer sausage (chopped)

Combine all meat ingredients together with desired amount of jalapeno peppers and half the crushed jalapeno and pork skin chips. Mix well with a small amount of hot water and cook 1-1/2 hours. Place cooked rice in a bowl topped with some more crushed jalapeno and pork skin chips. Pour gumbo mix over the rice. Serve with saltines or tortilla chips.

Serves: 6

> **DID YOU KNOW?** Work in and of itself helps to keep the camp calm and keeps issues down. "Plus, as the state has found, charging $15-50 per day while paying prisoners $2 per day is also quite profitable." (Texas prisoners are not paid.)

STUFFED POTATO

1 bag jalapeno chips (crushed)	1 package precooked beef
1/4 bottle jalapeno cheese	water
salsa (optional)	

Add water to chips and squish with hands to make into a paste. Remove 1/2 of potato paste from bag. Add precooked beef and cheese. Put the mixture you removed back on top and pat into a potato shape through the bag. Let cook for about an hour. Serve with tortilla chips. *Flavorful!*

Serves: 2

> **DID YOU KNOW?** Most Texas TDCJ units (prisons) have an inmate craft shop. The Mountain View Unit does not.

Spicy Potato Salad

1 package herb instant potatoes	1/2 bag jalapeno chips (crushed)
1/4 bag hot fries (crushed	1 package pickle (diced) (desired amount)
mustard (desired amount)	salad dressing (desired amount)
1 package chili seasoning (desired amount)	1 package jalapeno pepper (seeded and diced) (desired amount)

Combine potatoes, jalapeno chips, and hot fries with water to cook as instructed on package. Make mixture stiff. Add salad dressing, mustard, pickle, jalapeno pepper, and chili seasoning. Mix well and serve.

Serves: 2

DID YOU KNOW? The prison dentist ONLY pulls or fills teeth. An inmate can only have their teeth cleaned if they pass a plaque test with less than 10% plaque. If the inmate fails the plaque test, then the teeth are not cleaned.

Stuffed Ham

1/2 bag rice (cooked)	1 package chicken seasoning
1/4 bag jalapeno chips (crushed)	jalapeno cheese (desired amount)
butter (desired amount)	4 each dental flossers
2 packages processed meat singles (butterflied)	water

In a large bowl mix together cooked rice, jalapeno chips, chicken seasoning, butter, and water. On the inside of both butterflied processed meat, divide the rice mixture between the two portions. Close the stuffed meat and hold together with the dental flossers. Bag each serving individually. Divide the excess rice mixture between the two bags. Cook for 2 hours. ***Homestyle!***

Serves: 2

DID YOU KNOW? There are 112 prison units in the state of Texas comprised of more than 150,000 inmates.

Feast in a Bag

STUFFED PEPPERS

1 package tuna or precooked beef	4 tablespoons jalapeno cheese
1 sleeve saltine crackers	1/2 cup rice
1 package chicken seasoning (for tuna) or beef seasoning (for precooked beef)	6 packages jalapeno peppers (seeded)

Cook rice with seasoning. Once rice is cooked add the meat and cheese and cook for one hour. Clean out jalapeno peppers leaving them whole. Stuff cooked mixture into jalapeno peppers. Serve with saltine crackers and any left over mixture.

Serves: 2

DID YOU KNOW? "For several decades, the federal docket has been crowded with prisoner challenges to conditions of confinement. To stem this perceived flood of frivolous litigation, Congress enacted the Prison Litigation Reform Act of 1996."
The Columbia Law Review

SUMMER SAUSAGE SANDWICH

1 package summer sausage (sliced)	2 tablespoons jalapeno cheese
2 tablespoons salad dressing	4 slices bread

Spread cheese on 2 slices of bread and then spread the salad dressing on the other 2 slices. Place sliced summer sausage on top of either piece of bread with cheese or with salad dressing. Top with other piece of bread. ***Enjoy!***

Serves: 2

DID YOU KNOW? Even though Capital Punishment has been abolished in most of the industrialized world, Texas with less than 10 percent of the nation's population accounts for about half of this country's executions.
Source: *Dallas Morning News*, August 27, 2009

STUFFED SAUSAGE

1/2 bag rice	2 packages summer sausages
1 package beef seasoning	1/2 bag jalapeno chips (crushed)
1 package jalapeno peppers (seeded & diced)	1 tablespoon instant potatoes (any flavor)
	water

Rice: Precook rice with seasoning packet.

Sausages: Hollow out sausages by cutting off both ends and using your spoon to carve out meat (without tearing skin). Set casing aside.

Chop sausage meat up into tiny pieces. Add diced jalapeno pepper. Mix in desired amount of cheese, 1/2 bag of jalapeno chips, 1 spoon of instant potatoes. Add precooked rice along with desired amount of water (this adds moisture to rice when cooking in sausage).

Stuff sausage casing with rice mixture. Place remaining rice mixture in bag with the two stuffed sausages in the center of rice in the bag.

Double bag and cook at least 2 hours.

Serves: 2

DID YOU KNOW? Visitors are not allowed to photograph buildings, fences, or any other part of the prison unit.

SWEET-N-SOUR SANDWICHES

1 package mackerel or tuna	8 slices bread
2 tablespoons salad dressing	1/2 package pickle (chopped)
1 tablespoon mustard	2 each sweeteners
2 tablespoons salsa	1 tablespoon strawberry preserves
2 packages jalapeno peppers (seeded & diced)	1 tablespoon bbq sauce

Combine all the ingredients except the bread. Mix well. Place mixture on bread slices to create sandwiches. *Yowza!*

Serves: 4

DID YOU KNOW? Texas prisoners do not receive conjugal visits.

SUPER LAYERED NACHOS

1 package summer sausage (diced)	1 package chili with beans
1/4 bag refried beans	1/4 pickle (diced)
1/2 bottle jalapeno cheese	salsa (desired amount)
tortilla chips	hot water

   Place diced summer sausage in cooking bag and let cook. Add water to refried beans to hydrate. Add hydrated beans and desired amount of cheese to chili. Stir and let cook for 1 hour. Place remaining cheese in a cooking bag and let melt. Pour bean with chili mix over tortilla chips. Pour summer sausage on top. Pour melted cheese on top. Pour salsa on top. Pour diced pickles on top. **Makes a meal!**
   Serves: 2

> **Did YOU KNOW?** Inmates are allowed to display one photograph on the table that is attached to their bunk in their cubicle.

SWEET & SOUR TUNA SALAD

2 packages chicken soup	1 package tuna
1 tablespoon salad dressing	1/2 package pickle (cut up)
2 packages peach drink mix	hot water
2 packages jalapeno peppers (seeded & diced)	

1. Cook noodles then pour into a large bowl
2. Add both chicken seasoning packs, pickle, diced jalapeno pepper, salad dressing, tuna, and drink mix.
3. Mix then serve with crackers

VARIATION: Tuna Salad
Leave out the drink mix for plain tuna salad.
Serves: 3

> **DID YOU KNOW?** Inmates can share food in the chow hall as long as they are seated at the same table. They are not allowed to share food in the dorm even if they are seated at the same table in the dorm.

TAMALES

1 bag corn chips (crushed)	1/2 bottle jalapeno cheese
2 packages chili seasoning	hot water
1 package meat of your choice	

Get several sheets of paper or strips of a brown sack from the commissary and tear into at least 4x4 strips. Pour crushed corn chips into bowl. Add chili seasoning and mix well. Pour water onto corn chip mixture and stir. Keep adding water and stir until you have a very moist paste. Take a heaping spoonful of mixture and place on center of paper strip. With your hands mash and spread out to make a round or oval shape. Squeeze cheese into middle and spread. Add 1/2 spoonful of meat and spread evenly. Take one side of your paper and fold in half. Fold other side over so that the tamale is closed. Mold with your hands sealing tamale. Fold paper around tamale and add to cooking bag. Let cook an hour. Serve with salsa or guacamole. (See guacamole recipe on page 56.) *Ole'!*

Serves: 3-4

DID YOU KNOW? If an inmate is in their cubicle, in the shower, or using the toilet, their cubicle does not have to be in compliance. But, as soon as the inmate enters the dayroom, the cubicle must be in compliance or risk receiving a disciplinary case.

TOMATO SOUP

2 tablespoons powdered milk	1-2 tablespoon ketchup
1 each tomato juice	

Heat tomato juice in container. Mix powered milk with 2 tablespoons hot water slowly to avoid lumps and add to tomato juice. Add ketchup and stir. Serve with sandwiches or cheese nips. *Savory!*

Serves: 2

DID YOU KNOW? Inmates are allowed to wear sunglasses at recreation. The only problem is that TDCJ doesn't sell them to the inmates. So…could of, would of, should of…

Feast in a Bag

TANGY & CRUNCHY TUNA SALAD

1 package tuna	1 package trail mix
2-3 tablespoons salad dressing	2-3 tablespoons sunflower seeds
1/2 cup jalapeno chips (crushed)	1 tablespoon pickle (chopped)
2 packages chicken soup	2 packages peach drink mix
1 package jalapeno pepper (seeded & diced))	1 package lemon drink mix

Cook noodles until done. Pour into bowl and add all ingredients. Mix well. Serve with crackers on the side.

Serves: 2

DID YOU KNOW? When the female inmates are sent to the prison hospital in Galveston; they stay over 2 or more nights at the Goree male unit in Huntsville. The Goree unit is designated to house male inmates that are enrolled in the sex offender program. The females are housed right below the male sex offenders.

TRADITIONAL TUNA SANDWICH WITH ZEST

1 package tuna	1/8 bag jalapeno chips (crushed)
1/8 package pickle (diced)	1 tablespoon pickle juice
3-4 tablespoon salad dressing or sandwich spread	salt & pepper to taste
	4 slices of bread

Combine all ingredients and mix them thoroughly. Add desired amount of salt and pepper. Spoon mixture onto bread, top with additional slice of bread. Serve with chips. *Enjoy!*

Serves: 2

DID YOU KNOW? TDCJ does not issue dentures. If an inmate does not have any teeth or dentures (come in with them) then they gum their food or they do not eat.

TUNA BALL

1 package tuna	1/4 bottle jalapeno cheese
1/2 bag rice	1/4 bag jalapeno chips (crushed)
1 package flour tortillas	1 sleeve butter crackers (crushed)
6 packages jalapeno peppers (seeded & diced)	1 package chicken or chili seasoning

In a bowl add tuna, cooked rice, crushed jalapeno chips, 1/2 the seasoning pack and a few squirts of cheese. Mix and form into a big ball. In another bowl crush the snack crackers and add the rest of the seasoning pack. Coat the tuna ball in cheese then roll it in the cracker mixture.

Lay out jalapeno slivers, warm flour tortillas and set out crackers. ***Bon Appetite!***

Serves: 2-3

> **DID YOU KNOW?** Texas is ranked #1 in death-row executions.

TUNA BOAT

1 package tuna	1 sleeve crackers
1 each pickle	2-3 teaspoons sandwich spread
2 teaspoons jalapeno chips (crushed)	1/4 teaspoon ketchup
2-3 teaspoons sunflower seeds (if desired)	2 teaspoons salsa verde chips (crushed)

Cut pickle in half lengthwise and scrape out the seeds with spoon and discard them.

In a bowl mix tuna with sandwich spread. Add crushed chips and mix well. Add ketchup and mix. Add sunflower seeds, if desired and mix well. Spoon mixture equally into pickle halves and serve with crackers.

Serves: 2

> **DID YOU KNOW?** Shorts and cutoffs are not allowed to be worn by visitors when coming to visit an inmate.

TUNA TACOS

1 package flour tortillas	1 package chicken seasoning
1 package tuna	5 packages cream cheese
1/2 bag rice (cooked)	1/2 bottle jalapeno cheese
1/4 bag jalapeno chips (crushed)	

In a bowl mix rice, tuna, jalapeno chips and chicken seasoning packet. Take a flour tortilla and spread cream cheese and jalapeno cheese on it. Then put 1-2 tablespoons of tuna/rice mixture in the center of flour tortilla, then fold and put in cooking bag and cook for 1-2 hours.

Serves: 3

> **DID YOU KNOW?** Inmates are only allowed to take a comb or brush, handkerchief, and ID card into their workplace. Most state inmates in Texas receive no pay for their work.

TUNA WRAPS

1 package tuna	1 package chicken seasoning
1/4 bag rice	2 tablespoons salsa
6 flour tortillas	1 tablespoon jalapeno cheese
1 package chili seasoning	hot water

Combine tuna, salsa, chili seasoning, chicken seasoning, rice, and cheese into a bowl. Add a little hot water to hydrate rice. Stir well. Spread cheese on tortillas and add tuna mixture. Roll into a tortilla wrap and place in your cooking bag. Let cook about an hour. ***Dig in!***

Serves: 2

> **DID YOU KNOW?** Wrongfully imprisoned people in the state of Texas receive up front payments of $80,000 per year incarcerated. They also get a lifetime annuity worth the same amount, but paid out monthly. Payments can be made to survivors.
> Source: *Dallas Morning News*, April 25, 2009

TUNA WRAPS, TWO!

1 package flour tortillas	3 tablespoons sandwich spread
1 package tuna	1 cup jalapeno cheese
1/4 package dill pickle (chopped)	1/4 cup salsa verde chips (crushed)
1 package jalapeno pepper (seeded & diced)	

In a bowl mix tuna, sandwich spread, pickle pieces, crushed chips and jalapeno pepper pieces.

In center of flour tortillas; spoon 2 or 3 spoonfuls of tuna mixture and fold in half or roll as a burrito. Makes a total of 4 wraps with the tuna mixture. Place wraps/burritos in bag and heat 30 – 40 minutes. Add cheese on top.

VARIATIONS:
Squeeze cheese inside wrap on top of tuna mixture then heat.
Add trail mix or energizer mix to tuna mixture for a nutty or fruity taste.
Mix sandwich spread, squeeze cheese, and salsa and pour over wraps/burritos after they are heated and before eating.
Serves: 2

DID YOU KNOW? Inmates are not allowed to use a grievance form to comment on the effectiveness and credibility of the grievance procedure.

ZESTY TUNA TACOS

1 package tuna	4 tablespoons jalapeno chips (crushed)
3 tortillas	1/4 package pickle (diced)
4 tablespoon jalapeno cheese	salt & pepper (to taste)

Combine ingredients in a bowl. Mix until well blended. Divide mixture evenly onto the 3 tortillas. Fold as tacos. ***Ole!***
Serves: 2

DID YOU KNOW? Inmates are not allowed to talk in the bedroom (living) area and are not allowed to talk in front of the T.V. They haven't quite figured out where in the dorm they are allowed to talk.

Feast in a Bag

YUMMY MEXICAN TACOS

1 package precooked beef	1 package chili seasoning
9 tortillas	salsa (desired amount)
1/2 bag refried beans	jalapeno cheese (desired amount)
1 package jalapeno pepper (seeded & diced)	

Make beans thick with 1/2 chili package; heat precooked beef with the other 1/2 chili package and add cut up peppers. Heat tortillas and place a spoonful of beans on top and spread. Then add a spoonful of precooked beef, a squirt cheese with salsa on top of tortilla; fold in half and eat.

Serves: 3

DID YOU KNOW? At state prisons around the country, jailed women are routinely shackled during childbirth, often by correctional staff without medical training, according to civil rights organizations and prisoner advocates.

ZESTY/TANGY NACHOS

1/2 package refried beans	2 tablespoons bbq sauce
1 package tortilla chips	1/4 bottle jalapeno cheese
1/2 package rice	1/2 package pickle (cut-up)
1 package jalapeno pepper (seeded & diced)	1 package chili seasoning
	1/2 bottle salsa

Prepare beans in insert, add pickle, jalapeno cheese, bbq sauce, and cook in hot pot for 30 min. In separate insert or cooking jar, prepare rice with water and add chili seasoning.

Layer chips in large bowl. Pour bean mixture over chips then cover with rice. Top off with salsa and jalapeno. *Yummy!*

Serves: 4

DID YOU KNOW? Inmates must exchange razors on a one for one basis. Female offenders can exchange razors only on the 1st and 3rd Monday of every month.

All Purpose Cheese Sauce

1/2 bottle jalapeno cheese	1 bag powdered milk
1/2 bottle salsa	hot water

Combine powdered milk and add hot water slowly to avoid lumps. Add jalapeno cheese and stir until smooth. Add salsa and stir. Let cook one hour.
Serves: 3

> **DID YOU KNOW?** However the basic facts of her case will remain unchanged. …it will continue on as a case study for how easily the reliance on gossip and innuendo by the police, prosecutors, witnesses, judge and jurors involved in a case can result in an out of control murder prosecution that takes on a life of its own.
> *Kirstin Blaise Lobato's Unreasonable Conviction* by Hans Sherrer

All Round Dip

1 bottle salad dressing	1 package chili seasoning
1 bottle salsa or picante sauce	

Mix all ingredients and serve with everything from chips to burritos. It will keep for days.
Serves: 4

> **DID YOU KNOW?** Senator Jim Webb of Virginia has proposed a National Commission to study the American Criminal Justice System and correct its flaws. As originally proposed the commission membership did not include prisoner advocates, former prisoners, the wrongfully convicted, or prison rights organizations.
> Source: www.wrongful-convictions.blogspot.com/2009/07/gloria-killian-for-national-prison.html

BBQ Bean Dip

1/2 bag refried beans (precooked)	1 tablespoon BBQ sauce
2 tablespoons pickles (diced)	3 dashes salt (seasoned)

Mix together in large bowl the pre-cooked beans, pickles, bbq sauce, and seasoned salt. Cook for 30 minutes. *Deliciously mouth-watering!*
Serves: 2

> **DID YOU KNOW?** Inmates buy items from the commissary that are made by other inmates at their assigned jobs such as T-shirts, panties, greeting cards, etc. These items are made with free labor from the inmates and then sold back to inmates through the unit's commissary and are paid for by the inmates family.

Bean Dip

1 bag refried beans	1 dash hot sauce
1/2 bag jalapeno chips	1 package jalapenos (seeded & diced)
1 tablespoon jalapeno cheese	4 tablespoons salsa

Cook beans according to package instructions. Add the rest of the ingredients and let cook 10 minutes until mixture is thick. Serve with tortilla chips.
Serves: 2

> **DID YOU KNOW?** Even if an officer gives an inmate a direct order that is not a written or posted rule, the inmate still has to do what ever that officer says or the inmate can be written up for disobeying a direct order. The inmate can also receive disciplinary punishment.

Butter Pickles

1 package pickle (cut in chunks)	4 each peach drink mix
1 each lemon drink mix	

Cut pickle into chunks and put in jar with pickle juice. Add lemon and peach drink mix and shake. Let set for 2 days.

Serves: 6-8

> **DID YOU KNOW?** In September 2009, a TDCJ death row chaplain was facing dismissal after he acknowledged smuggling out letters for a condemned inmate who used these letters to post internet messages threatening a State Senator and his family.

Cheese Dip

1/2 bottle jalapeno cheese	1/2 bottle salsa
1 bag tortilla chips	1 1/2 package chili seasoning
1 package summer sausage (chopped)	1 package processed meat single (chopped)

Mix salsa and cheese in a bag. Add small pieces of meat singles and sausage with 1/2 package of seasoning to cheese mixture and mix again. Cook for 1-1/2 hours. Add 1 package of seasoning to tortilla chip bag until all chips are seasoned. Serve chips with dip.

Serves: 2

> **DID YOU KNOW?** Of the eleven thousand cases of alleged prosecutorial misconduct examined by the Center for Public Integrity, the appellate courts reversed convictions, dismissed charges, or reduced sentences in just over two thousand.
> *Arbitrary Justice: The Power of the American Prosecutor* by Angela J. Davis

CHIPOLTE MAYO

1 each lemon drink mix	2 packages chili seasoning
1 jar salad dressing	

Combine all ingredients in salad dressing jar and stir. ***Enjoy!***
Serves: 6-8

> **DID YOU KNOW?** The Board of Criminal Justice is made up of nine (9) unpaid citizens. They are appointed by the governor of Texas.

CREAMY BUTTER BEANS

1/2 bag refried beans	2 tablespoons jalapeno cheese
1 tablespoon salad dressing	hot water

Add desired amount of hot water to beans and stir. Add all other ingredients and stir well. Let cook 30-45 minutes.
Serves: 3

> **DID YOU KNOW?** Inmates are not allowed to have extreme hairstyles. No Mohawk, "tailed," or shaved/partially-shaved heads are allowed.

CREAMY CHOCONILLA DRINK

4 tablespoons hot chocolate	1 each french vanilla cappuccino
6 tablespoons powdered milk	hot water

Mix everything into your mug or cup. Add water and stir well and serve with cookies.
Serves: 1

> **DID YOU KNOW?** The female youth offenders are housed on the same unit (Hilltop) as the female sex offenders.

DIP-N-LICK

1 each fruit stick	1 each empty jar (preferably small)
10-15 packages of your favorite drink mix – combine the flavors.	

Open and pour drink mix into a jar. Open fruit stick and wet in your mouth. Insert fruit stick into jar and swirl around getting the mixture on fruit stick. Eat the part of the fruit stick with drink mixture. *Yum!*
Serves: 1

DID YOU KNOW? If an inmate commits a crime that requires them to be housed in protective custody, **each** of these inmates at Mt. View are treated to a **flat screen T.V.** with remote. But, if an inmate lives in general population, then 34 women share a T.V. The guard controls the remote control. The channel is changed on the hour, but only if the officer feels like doing it. The volume is too low most of the time and the close captioning stays jumbled. To top it off, at certain times of the day, the glare through the tall, curtainless windows further blocks the view of the TV screen.

FAUX SANGRIA'

1 each strawberry soda	ice
1 each orange sports drink packet	

Pour the soda over ice in 2 tall glasses. Mix half of the sports drink mix packet in each glass and stir well.
Serves: 2

DID YOU KNOW? Nationally known private investigator Martin Yant wrote in his book *Presumed Guilty*: "When innocent people are wrongly convicted, that wrongful conviction is often the result of a bungled police investigation worthy of the Keystone Cops."
Kirstin Blaise Lobato's Unreasonable Conviction by Hans Sherrer

GUACAMOLE

3-4 tablespoons salad dressing	1 bag salsa verde chips (crushed fine)
1 package lemon drink mix	4 tablespoons salsa
1/2 package jalapeno (seeded & diced)	

Combine crushed salsa verde chips, jalapeno, salsa, and salad dressing in bowl. Mix well. Add more salad dressing and/or salsa if needed. It should be a very moist paste. Sprinkle lemon drink mix a little at a time and mix. Taste and add more drink mix if needed. Serve with tortilla chips or with your Mexican plate. ***Enjoy!***

Serves: 2

> **DID YOU KNOW?** 39-year-old Anthony Miller robbed a bank in Pennsylvania because he said, "Prison is preferable to marriage." Miller approached tellers with a BB gun, asked for money and told them to call the police. Miller even asked the tellers for updates on their efforts to reach authorities.

HOMEMADE SALSA

1/4 package pickle (diced)	1 package chili seasoning
1 each tomato juice	1/2 bottle salsa
1 package jalapeno (seeded & diced)	2 dash hot sauce

Combine all ingredients into empty jar. Stir well. Taste and add more of anything that you think needs to be added. Serve with tortilla chips or eat with your Mexican plate or on nachos.

Serves: 8

> **DID YOU KNOW?** A child molester faked his own death and almost got away with it after the Travis County (Austin, Texas) medical examiner mistook the burned body of an 81-year-old woman for the 23-year-old man.
> Source: *Ft. Worth Star Telegram*, September 26, 2009.

ITALIAN ICE

6 each rainbow popcicles	1/2 each strawberry/kiwi juice
1/4 bottle strawberry preserves	

Use any desired fruit from fruit pies (cherry, peach, strawberry or pineapple) can be substituted for strawberry preserves. In a large bowl or hot pot, break up popsicles. Add strawberry/kiwi juice and fruit. Mix until it makes a smooth icy slush.

Serves: 3

> **DID YOU KNOW?** We've all heard of programs like "Scared Straight" that give young offenders a glimpse into prison life. Now Missouri Senator Tim Green proposes a law. The proposed bill would require students tour prisons.
> KFVS – Cape Girardeau, MO, February 8, 2007

MACKEREL SOAKS

To rid mackerel of the awful fishy smell and taste – first rinse it several times then let it soak in the following mixture:

1 package of mackerel	1 teaspoon of salt
1 entire juice from a pickle	water (desired amount)

Let the mackerel soak for 30 minutes then rinse well.
Try eating with just salsa on top with a cracker.
You'll be pleasantly surprised!

> **DID YOU KNOW?** TDCJ is only required to provide the inmates with the OPPORTUNITY to have a clean shower towel at least three (3) times per week.

Mexican Snacks

2 flour tortillas	1 package chili seasoning
1/2 cup refried beans	jalapeno cheese (desired amount)
1 bag nacho chips (crushed)	1/2 package salsa verde chips (crushed)
1 package chili with beans	

Cook beans with chili seasoning. Don't make runny. Heat chili with beans. In a large bowl, lay one tortilla on the bottom of the bowl. Pour bean mixture on top then place both chips (crushed) on top. Lay 2nd tortilla on top and cover with chili with bean mixture. Apply desired cheese on top.

Serves: 1

> **DID YOU KNOW?** Nearly 10% of all prisoners nationally in 2008 are serving a life sentence.
> Source: *The New York Times*

Munch'n Mix

1/2 bag party mix	2 each candy bars (any flavor)
1/2 bag corn chips	1 bag plain peanuts
1 bag caramel popcorn or cheese popcorn	1 bag M&M candy

Melt candy bars in jar or insert. Mix chips, popcorn, nuts and M&M candy in a large bowl. Drizzle melted candy bars over mixture and toss lightly. Let "set" until candy re-hardens. Plain chocolate candy bar works best, but any flavor will do. ***Enjoy!***

Serves: 2

> **DID YOU KNOW?** Inmates are allowed to check-out 3 books each week from the unit library. But, no inmate is allowed to check-out 2 books from the same author.

Snacks, Dips, and More

Peach Habenero Salsa

4 each peach pies (remove peaches)	1 bottle habenero sauce
10 package jalapeno peppers (seeded & chopped)	

In large bowl, mix peaches and jalapeno peppers. Add desired amount of habenero sauce. Eat with desired chips.

Serves: 4

> **DID YOU KNOW?** In November 2009 the U.S. Supreme Court tossed out convicted murderer George Porter's death sentence because his Florida jury wasn't told of the Korean War vets' combat-induced post traumatic stress syndrome.
>
> "Our nation has a long tradition of according leniency to veterans in recognition of their service, especially for those who fought on the front lines as Porter did," said the Supreme Court in its opinion.
> *The Associated Press* by Paul Elias - May 23, 2010

Pin Wheels

1 package flour tortillas	10 packages cream cheese
2 packages jalapenos (remove seeds & cut into slivers)	1/4 bottle salsa

On each tortilla spread cream cheese. Top with desired amount of salsa and slivers of jalapenos. Roll into a wrap. ***Enjoy!***

Serves: 3

> **DID YOU KNOW?** Only inmates that are walking directly to and from the water fountain in the dayroom can be dressed in their nightgown or shorts and a t-shirt. Even though the trashcan is also in the dayroom, walking to it dressed in a gown would get the inmate a disciplinary case.

POPCORN BALL

1 bag carmel popcorn	2 each Snickers candy bars
2 tablespoons butter (heat in insert)	

Empty popcorn into large white bowl then pour butter over popcorn and stir to coat evenly. Melt the candy bar in an insert. When melted, stir into popcorn and mold into ball.

Serves: 1 large ball

☺ **HELPFUL HINT!!**: If the ball isn't molding as you want, use a little hot chocolate syrup and add as needed.

> **DID YOU KNOW?** If an inmate does not have their ID card with them, it is considered a refusal or failure to obey orders. There are no accidents, "I forgots," or mistakes in prison. All actions are considered as deliberate and subject to disciplinary consequences.

POPCORN KRISPIES

1 bag carmel popcorn	2 tablespoons butter
3 each Milky Way candy bars (melted)	1 bag M&M candy

Crush carmel popcorn as small as you can. Mix in a bag the melted candy bars, popcorn, and M&M candy. Mash around in bag until well mixed up. Flatten inside bag to make a thin brick. Let set for an hour.

Serves: 3

> **DID YOU KNOW?** An indigent inmate may use indigent postage (paid by TDCJ) to send five (5) one-ounce domestic letters per week to general correspondents and five (5) items to legal correspondents. An indigent inmate has less than $5 in their trust fund account.

Potato Salad

1 bag instant potatoes	mustard (desired amount)
1/2 package pickle (diced)	water (desired amount)
jalapeno chips (crushed) (desired amount)	1 package chili seasoning (desired amount)
salad dressing (desired amount)	

Make mashed potatoes thick. Add minced pickle, desired amount of salad dressing, mustard, and chili packet. Garnish with crushed jalapeno chips.

Serves: 4

> **DID YOU KNOW?** More prisoners than ever (almost 9,000 in Texas) are serving life terms. They are straining corrections budgets at a time when financially strapped states are struggling to cut costs.
> Source: *The New York Times*

Rainbow Slushies

2 each rainbow popsicles
1 each lemon-lime soda

Mix in insert until slushie.

VARIATIONS: Substitute any flavored soda in place of the lemon lime soda.

Serves: 2

> **DID YOU KNOW?** In October 2008, when a convicted murderer on death-row used a cell phone to make threatening phone calls to a Texas state senator, prison officials blamed it on prison guards because they are under paid and easily corrupted.
> Source: *Dallas Morning News*, October 22, 2008

Ranch Dip/Sandwich Spread

1 package ranch dressing	2 package cream cheese

Put cream cheese in bowl and mix ranch dressing until it's creamy. It's a wonderful dip and it tastes yummy mixed with tuna fish!
Serves: 2

> **DID YOU KNOW?** Call to cut UK prison population, 5,000 inmates should be in mental health units while another 5,000 should be in drug rehab centers. *BBC News*, May 8, 2008

Relish

1 package pickle (minced)	1 package chicken seasoning
2 packages jalapeno peppers (seeded & diced)	1/2 bottle salsa

Mix all ingredients together.

> **DID YOU KNOW?** An inmate is allowed to spend $85 at the prison commissary every two (2) weeks, providing their family puts the money into a non-interest bearing account with TDCJ.

Sandwich Mustard Dressing

1 package chili seasoning	1 jar mustard

Mix together.

> **DID YOU KNOW?** 3-G inmates (inmates with charges that are aggravated) receive no good conduct time or credit for work time. They must complete their sentence day-for-day because good conduct time and work-time are considered a privilege and not a right.

Snacks, Dips, and More

Sandwich Dressings

| 1 package seasoning packet (any flavor) | 1 jar salad dressing |

Mix seasoning into salad dressing.

☺ **VARIATION**: Tuna Sandwiches – salad dressing and chicken seasoning.

Pork Skin Sandwiches – salad dressing and chili seasoning.

> **DID YOU KNOW?** As of April 1, 2004, ALL inmates are required to submit to a DNA test, if a sample has not been previously obtained.

Simple Rice

1/2 bag rice	1/2 package chili seasoning
1/8 bag jalapeno chips (crushed)	hot water
1/2 package chicken seasoning	

Combine above ingredients into cooking bag with 1-1/2 to 2 cups of hot water and stir well. Cook 45 minutes and serve.

Serves: 4

> **DID YOU KNOW?** Inmates shall be provided the OPPORTUNITY to have three complete sets of clean clothing per week.

Soy Sauce

| 1 package beef seasoning | 1/4 cup hot water |
| 1/4 tablespoon coffee | |

Mix together.
Enjoy on rice or chicken!

> **DID YOU KNOW?** Texas inmates may not embellish their outgoing envelopes with illustrations or written messages other than the return address.

SPANISH RICE

1/2 bag rice (desired portion)	salt and pepper (to taste)
1 each tomato juice	1 package jalapeno (seeded & diced)
2 tablespoons jalapeno cheese	

Mix all ingredients with enough tomato juice to cover. Cook until done. Fluff and serve.

Serves: 2

DID YOU KNOW? America imprisons 756 inmates per 100,000 residents, a rate nearly five times the world's average. About one in every 31 adults in this country is in jail or on supervised release. Either we are the most evil people on earth or we are doing something very wrong. Source: *Waco Tribune/Herald*, March 29, 2009

SPANISH RICE, TWO!

1/2 bag rice	1 package chili seasoning
1/2 cup salsa	butter (desired amount)
1 each tomato juice (spicy if desired)	3 tablespoons water
1/2 summer sausage or 1 processed meat singles	1 package jalapeno peppers (seeded & diced)

Mix rice, seasoning, and salsa in bowl. Cut up peppers and meat in small pieces. Mix into mixture of rice. In a bag, add all ingredients with 1/2 the tomato juice and a squirt of butter. Add 3 tablespoons of water. Place bag in hot pot and heat for an hour.

Serves: 2

DID YOU KNOW? Richard Winfrey Sr. was convicted of murder in 2007 based on his scent being picked by a dog during a lineup. The Texas Court of Criminal Appeals overturned his conviction and barred his retrial in September 2010 when it ruled the dog scent evidence was unreliable. Austin *American-Statesman*, September 22, 2010.

SWEET-N-SPICY RICE

1 bag rice	1 each orange/pineapple juice
1 each mango drink mix	3 each sweeteners
1 package chili seasoning	1 package fruit nut mix
1 package jalapeno pepper (seeded and diced) (desired amount)	

Combine rice, juice, drink mix, jalapeno pepper, sweeteners and fruit nut mix. Cook 1 1/2 hours. Pour into a bowl and sprinkle with chili seasoning to taste.

Serves: 4

> **DID YOU KNOW?** In 1999, the Supreme Court ruled that it was a violation of the Fourth Amendment for media to record police during a raid into a private residence.
> *The Associated Press* By Corey Williams and Jeff Karoub, May 21, 2010

SWEET & SOUR PICKLES

1 package pickle
1 package drink mix (any flavor, or spoonfuls of drink mixture from the Dip-n-Lick on page 55)

Simply pour drink mixture on top of pickle. ***Enjoy!***
Serves: 1

> **DID YOU KNOW?** Today, scientists can create DNA profiles from a speck of blood the size of a pinhead and gather evidence from things people have merely touched, such as a knife handle or a steering wheel. So called "touch" DNA can come from sources including skin cells, sweat, and saliva.
> *Ventura County Star* by Adam Foxman May 23, 2010

SWEET & TANGY MUSTARD

1 jar mustard	2 each drink mixes (any flavor)
1 package chili seasoning	2 each sweeteners

Combine all ingredients in the mustard jar and stir. *Wow!*
Serves: 6-8

DID YOU KNOW? In Texas, convicts are not even allowed to see their own files and, until recently, could not see documents to which they had to respond as the parole board considered their release.
Source: *Austin American-Statesman* "Parole policies under fire," September 2009

☺ **HELPFUL HINT!** We try to keep trail mix on hand and keep the almonds. This way we can use as needed, already crushed.

SWEET MAYO

1 jar salad dressing
4 each sweeteners

Combine ingredients in salad dressing jar and stir.
Serves: 6-8

DID YOU KNOW? On February 6, 2008, Massachusetts U.S. Bankruptcy Judge Robert Somma, 63, was pulled over following a minor car accident and charged with driving while intoxicated. He was wearing high heels, stockings and a cocktail dress at the time, and the arresting officer noted that the judge had to retrieve his driver's license from his purse.
Source: *Prison Legal News*, August 2009

Sweet Rice Casserole

1/4 bag rice	1 tablespoon butter
1 package trail mix	1 tablespoon peanut butter
1-2 packages sweeteners	2 tablespoons powdered milk
hot water	

Mix all ingredients with enough water to cover. Stir often while cooking, and add water if necessary. Mixture should be moist and juicy, but not soupy.

Serves: 2

> **DID YOU KNOW?** Alabama Circuit Court Judge Herman Thomas, resigned in October 2007, after being accused of paddling or whipping male prisoners on their buttocks and making them perform sex acts in a small storage closet (room in his judicial chambers, where semen stains were found).
> Source: *Prison Legal News*, February 2008

1001 Island Dressing

1 jar salad dressing	1/2 package pickle (minced and desired amount)
ketchup (desired amount)	

Mix all ingredients together.
Serves: 6-8

> **DID YOU KNOW?** Texas Court of Criminal Appeals Judge Sharon Keller, faced ethics charges because she prevented attorney's for a death row prisoner from filing a last-minute after-hours appeal, resulting in his execution.
> Source: *Prison Legal News*, August 2009

Almond Joyous Cake

almonds from trail mix (crushed)	1/4 cup powdered milk
8 each coconut macaroon cookies	1/2 cup hot chocolate mix
1 teaspoon butter	water
1 package chocolate crème cookies (save plastic cookie holder) (crushed)	1 each plain chocolate candy bar or 2 each chocolate with almonds candy bars

Separate cookie from filling and crush. Toss cookie crumbs with just enough butter to coat. Melt 1/2 of the hot chocolate mix in an insert cup with hot water to make about 1/4 cup of syrupy cocoa. Use as much or little of the syrup as needed to dampen crumbs enough to form into bars in the cookie holder.

Crush macaroon cookies and place in the hot pot insert with powdered milk and hot water, enough to cover. Let it cook down. Then pour slowly, mixing as you pour into cookie filling. Be careful not to get too thin. If needed crush one or two more macaroon cookies into filling. Spread on cake. Melt chocolate candy bar(s) into leftover hot chocolate, adding more hot chocolate if needed and drizzle on top. Then top with crushed almonds. Let set.

Serves: 6

DID YOU KNOW? Texas inmates are assured ten (10) hours of law library access per week.

Any Flavor Pudding

1 pint ice cream (any flavor)
1 1/2 package powdered milk

Combine the 2 items together. The more milk you add the thicker and creamier the pudding.

Serves: 4

DID YOU KNOW? Inmates have to pay a $3 co-pay for medical and dental care.

APPLE STREUDEL

1 package vanilla cream cookies	3 packages apple cereal bars
2 each apple pies	1 tablespoon hot water
2 packages apple oatmeal	2 tablespoons butter

In a bowl, separate the vanilla cookie and the cream center. Set centers aside. In another bowl, crumble up the cereal bars and apple pies then add the apple oatmeal and butter. Crush vanilla cookies and add to mixture and cook in hot pot for one hour. Put the cream center in a cup and add hot water and cook. After one hour take mixture out of the hot pot and drizzle cream on top.

Serves: 3

> **DID YOU KNOW?** An inmate can only change their religious designation every 6 months, even though God has not put a time-limit on Christianity.

BANANA PUDDING

1 bag vanilla wafers	1 bag powdered milk
1 each banana novelty ice cream	5 each banana flavored Moon pies
1 pint banana nut ice cream (melted)	

Start out with one big bowl and place vanilla wafers on bottom of bowl. Crumble banana Moon pies on top of the layer of vanilla wafers. In a cooking bag pour in melted ice cream and add one bag of powder milk slowly to avoid lumps and novelty ice cream. Heat in hot pot for 1 hour. Then pour over crushed pies. Top with vanilla wafers. Pour more melted ice cream on top. Add another layer of vanilla wafers. Let set overnight until all liquid is absorbed. Cut and serve!

Serves: 4

> **DID YOU KNOW?** Texas prisoners only receive mail 5 days a week. They have no Saturday delivery.

Banana Nut Bread

1/2 package macaroon cookies (coarsely crushed)	2 packages banana whey powder
	2 packages oatmeal (maple brown sugar)
3/4 package vanilla crème cookies (crème removed & cookie coarsely crushed)	2 each pecan pies
	butter (desired amount)
	water

Save enough cookie crumbs to cover bottom of container and top of bread. Toss cookie crumbs and oatmeal with just enough butter to coat. Gently add banana whey. Add enough hot water to fold into the texture of bread dough.

Don't stir or mix!

Pinch pecan pies into bite size pieces and fold into dough. Pack lightly by spoonfuls into square container (tray cookies came in). Don't pack down. Add hot water to vanilla crème center to make a glaze and spread on top. Sprinkle remaining cookie crumbs on top. Let sit overnight.

Serves: 4

> **DID YOU KNOW?** Trusty status inmates can be "crackheads." But, if an inmate kills the crack dealer and their charge is aggravated, they don't get the "perks" like the trustees.

Black Cherry Delight

1 package black cherry drink mix	1 tablespoon banana whey mix
1 package oatmeal (maple brown sugar)	1 package trail mix

Mix oatmeal and one tablespoon of banana whey, trail mix, black cherry drink mix (1/2 package) with cold water. Let set for 5-10 minutes. Enjoy!

Serves: 1

> **DID YOU KNOW?** When an inmate is a convicted sex offender, their neighbors will receive a post card about the inmate after arriving in the community. Information will also be printed in the local newspaper.

Banana Pudding, Two!

1 bag vanilla wafers	2 each banana fudge novelties
5 each banana Moon (marshmallow) pies	1 pint banana nut ice cream (melted)
	water

Start out with 2 big bowls. Let the ice cream melt. Crumble pies while still in the package. Open all the pies and empty into a big bowl.

Add warm water and gradually add to the pies. Stir until it's a loose, pudding-like consistency. Line the second bowl with the vanilla wafers and pour half of the pie mixture on top. Add another layer of wafers and pour the rest of the pie mixture over them. Add another layer of wafers and pour the melted ice cream on top. Add one more layer of vanilla wafers. Let set overnight until all the liquid is absorbed. Cut & serve.

Serves: 8

DID YOU KNOW? Parole is a privilege and not a right.

Banana Split Cake

1 package vanilla crème cookies	8-10 teaspoons butter
1 package banana whey mix	water
7-10 teaspoons hot chocolate	7-10 tablespoons strawberry preserves
2 each strawberry pies (just the filling)	

Separate cookie from filling. Crush cookies into course crumbs. Put banana whey in about 1/4 – 1/2 inch of hot water in insert and heat.

Toss cookie crumbs in butter. Use enough hot water to dampen. Press into bowl. DO NOT GET TOO MOIST!

Mix cookie centers into banana whey. Spread on cake.

Take filling from 2 strawberry pies and mix with the strawberry jam. Mix well. Drop even spoonfuls on top of cake. Melt several spoons of hot chocolate in hot water to make thick syrup. Drizzle over all of the cake and let set.

Serves: 6

DID YOU KNOW? Inmates that participate in gangs are placed in administrative segregation.

BASIC CHEESECAKE

1 package graham crackers	4 each sweeteners
15 packages cream cheese	3 large bowls and 1 empty jar
1 package crème cookies (vanilla, strawberry or lemon)	hot water

Scrape filling from cookies into empty jar. Take half of the cookies and crush into crumbs in one bowl. Crush graham crackers into crumbs in another bowl. Mix crumbs together in one bowl; add water – less than 1 cup – mix into crumbs. Press and form crumbs into crust in bottom half of bowl. Put jar with cookie filling in hotpot to soften. In third bowl, squeeze cream cheese packets and add sweeteners – mix well. Take melted cookie fillings out of hotpot and stir. Add filling to cream cheese and mix well. Pour into pie crust and smooth. Let sit for about 6 hours or until firm. Cut into pie-shaped wedges and serve.

Serves: 8

☺ **BONUS**: Cherry Cheese Cake! Make cheese cake using vanilla crème cookies. Scrape filling from 3 cherry pies into empty peanut butter jar. Add a few spoonfuls of hot water and stir. Spread filling over top of cheese cake. Let set. Cut into wedge and serve.

> **DID YOU KNOW?** In *Herrera v. Collins*, 506 U.S. 809 (1992), Chief Justice Rehnquist stated that because "innocence" is not specifically mentioned in the Constitution, a claim of innocence does not arise to a constitutional level.
>
> With all due respect, neither does the Constitution specifically discuss abortion, adoption, marriage, false imprisonment, or incest, but each of these has been found to involve constitutional rights.
>
> *System Failure* by James F. Love IV

☺ **HELPFUL HINT!!**: Clean your floor before you cook unless you like hairy food!

For The Sweet Tooth

Basic Cheesecake, Two!

1 package vanilla cream cookies (do not separate – crush into small pieces)	1 pint ice cream (any flavor except diet)
2 packages powdered milk	5 packages cream cheese
7-8 almonds (crushed)	4 tablespoons milk (liquid)

Crust – In large bowl, dampen the crushed cookies with liquid milk to form a crust on the bottom and sides of the bowl.

Filling – In another bowl pour in the pint of melted ice cream and all the cream cheese. Add the dry powdered milk a little at a time whipping it with a spoon to an "airy" consistency. When it holds its shape and bubbles slightly, pour into crust. Sprinkle with crushed almonds on top.

Serves: 6

> **DID YOU KNOW?** Inmates are not allowed to talk after the lights are turned out in the dorm.

Birthday Surprise

1 package double fudge cookies	3 Chick-O-Sticks (or 1-1/2 Butterfinger candy bars)
1 package M&M candy	
2 mugs hot chocolate	water (desired amount)

Cake: In large bowl crush cookies (cream removed) with 2 crushed Chick-O-Sticks (or 1 crushed Butterfinger). Mix and mash with hot chocolate and 1/2 package of M&M candy.

Frosting: In an insert mix the cream from cookies with 1 Chick-O-Stick (or 1/2 Butterfinger), hot chocolate, and desired amount of water.

Layer in large bowl cake and frosting, frost top with remaining 1/2 package of crushed M&M candy.

Serves: 8

> **DID YOU KNOW?** Inmates can not miss a day of work without a "lay in" or a disciplinary case will be given.

For The Sweet Tooth

BLACK CHERRY CHEESE CAKE

1 package chocolate crème cookies	3 packages blackcherry drink mix
1/4 bag hot chocolate mix	3 packages powdered milk
2 each plain chocolate candy bars	3 each sweeteners
1/2 bottle strawberry jam	water
1 each lemon-lime soda	

Crust: Separate filling from cookies and put cookie filling in an insert cup. Crush cookies in a bowl. Add hot chocolate, sweeteners, and water. Combine and mix until you have desired consistency for crust.

Filling: In another bowl, mix milk, blackberry drink mix, and lemon-lime soda until smooth and thick. Pour over crust.

Topping: In the insert cup melt the chocolate candy bars with the cookie filling then add the strawberry jam and combine. Pour over the filling and set aside overnight.

Serves: 8

DID YOU KNOW? All inmate property must fit in a box provided by the state that is approximately 1.75 cubic feet, but shall not exceed 2.0 cubic feet.

CARAMEL LATTE

1 each Milky Way candy bar	2 tablespoons hot chocolate mix
1 package vanilla cappuccino	

Break up the Milky Way bar and place in a hot pot to melt. Add vanilla cappuccino and hot chocolate and fill to the top with hot water. Stir well.

Serves: 1

DID YOU KNOW? Houston's 14th Court of Appeals rejected the argument by high-profile attorney Dick DeGuerin that a doctor could not have exposed himself to an undercover cop because his 2.8-inch penis is too small to have been seen.
Source: "Size matters; Court: Nah," *Houston Chronicle*, August 19, 2008

BLACK FOREST CAKE

2 each cherry pies (separate filling)	1/2 cup hot chocolate
1 teaspoon butter	water
1 package chocolate crème cookies	

Separate cookies from filling and crush cookies. Melt ½ cup hot chocolate in 1/4 cup hot water to make syrup. Toss crumbs with enough butter to coat. Mix this with your syrup to make cake and add more water if needed.

Press into bowl. Mix cookie filling with 3 – 4 tablespoons of hot water to make frosting. Frost cake then heat cherry filling. When hot, drop cherry filling on cake in strips. Let set.

Serves: 6

DID YOU KNOW? Bush granted 200 requests for pardons and commutations during his eight years in office, compared with 406 by former President Reagan and 457 by former President Clinton.
Source: *Prison Legal News*, April 2009

BROWNIE CAKE

1 tablespoon peanut butter (heaping)	1 each plain chocolate candy bar (optional)
1 package double fudge cookies	

Separate cookie from filling and place cookie in a bowl. Crush cookies and make into cake then put into bag. Cook in insert for 30 minutes or more. Top with the filling that you cook in your insert with peanut butter and chocolate bar. Serve hot.

Serves: 6

DID YOU KNOW? The end of one of the Texas prison system's oldest practices: the long ride back to Huntsville for release for most convicts who are finishing their sentences.....prison officials are working to establish at least six regional centers where convicts will be released.
Source: *Austin American-Statesman*

Blondie Brownie

1 package vanilla crème cookies	1 cup hot chocolate mix
hot water (1/2-3/4 hot pot lid of water) adjust according to desired texture of brownie.	1 bag chocolate covered peanuts (melted)

Brownie: Separate cream from cookies and crush cookies. Add 1/2 bag melted chocolate covered peanuts, hot chocolate mix, and water together. Place in cookie bag and cook for 30 minutes.

Blondie Frosting: In insert, whip vanilla cream from cookies, 1/2 bag of chocolate covered peanuts and a couple spoons of hot water until smooth and creamy.

After cooking brownies for 30 minutes mash using bottom of a jar in a bowl to ensure the brownie mixture is thoroughly mixed and has the desired texture. If too wet add hot chocolate powder; if too dry add water.

Place brownies in cookie tray and frost.

Servies: 6

> **DID YOU KNOW?** When an inmate is addressing a staff member, the inmate's hands will be placed behind their back.

Chocolate Candy Cluster

5 each chocolate candy bars with almonds (melted)	3 each Chick-O-Sticks (crushed) (or 1-1/2 Butterfinger candy bars)
1 bag peanuts (crushed)	

In a large bowl, mix melted chocolate bars, Chick-O-Sticks, and peanuts. Once well mixed form desired size clusters and place them in front of a fan. A chocolate lovers dream!

Serves: 4

> **DID YOU KNOW?** All inmates receive testing that determines educational, psychological, and substance abuse treatment needs upon arriving in the system.

CHOCOLATE CHEESE CAKE

1 bottle chocolate syrup	2 packages powdered milk
1 pint chocolate ice cream (melted)	hot water
2 each plain chocolate candy bars (melted)	1 package double fudge cookies (crushed)

Pour melted ice cream into bowl. Slowly pour powdered milk into melted ice cream while stirring. Once both packages are mixed and there aren't any lumps, squeeze desired amount of chocolate syrup into mixture until mixture tastes very chocolaty. In separate bowl, pour very little hot water over crushed cookies and stir. Mixture should be moist. Add more water if needed. Pour ice cream mixture on top of cookie mixture and let set 6 hours. After six hours, drizzle with melted chocolate and chocolate syrup on top. ***Enjoy!***

Serves: 6

DID YOU KNOW? Television programming about the legal system, even real trials that are televisied, often serves to misinform the public. *Arbitrary Justice: The Power of the American Prosecutor* by Angela J. Davis

CHOCOLATE COVERED CHERRIES

4 tablespoons hot chocolate mix	hot water
1 package black cherry drink mix	

Mix both ingredients and add water. Stir well, and place in hot pot for 30 minutes. When finished, stir again, and serve. Smells and tastes just like chocolate covered cherries.

Serves: 1

DID YOU KNOW? In Severn, MD, a woman whose home was burglarized, as she stayed with her daughter, was shocked to realize that "every item" at a nearby yard sale came from the woman's house.
Source: *The Baltimore Sun*

CHOCOLATE CRÈME PIZZA

1 sleeve graham crackers	2 tablespoons chocolate syrup
2 tablespoons hot chocolate	butter (desired amount)
1/2 bottle chocolate syrup	water
1 package chocolate crème cookies	

Crush honey crackers and mix in hot chocolate and butter. Add a little hot water and stir; crust should be firm, not mushy. Spread chocolate syrup on bottom of crust. Remove cream from cookies. Break cookies in quarters. Pour half the bottle of syrup over cookies. Mix until cookie pieces are fully saturated. Pour mixture into pizza crust. Mix cream filling from cookie with water and drizzle on top of pizza.

Serves: 4

DID YOU KNOW? Inmates are not allowed to eat food or candy while exiting their housing area.

CHOCOLATE LOVERS DREAM ... WITH ICE CREAM

8 each chocolate chip cookies	1 pint vanilla ice cream
1/4 jar peanut butter	1 package salted peanuts
4 each chocolate Moon pies	1/2 cup chocolate syrup

Mix vanilla ice cream and peanut butter until creamy. Take the marshmallow out of the Moon pie and place on top of chocolate chip cookie. Sprinkle peanuts on top of marshmallow. Put peanut butter ice cream on top of marshmallow then cover with second chocolate chip cookie. Mix the outside of the Moon pie with chocolate syrup and heat for 30 minutes. Drizzle over cookie.

Serves: 4

DID YOU KNOW? If an inmate participates in a vote to watch a specific television program, it must be watched by the voting inmates in its' entirety.

Chocolate & Mint Cookies

1 package chocolate crème cookies	hot water
2 each peppermint sticks (crushed fine)	

Remove cream from cookies and put in a bowl. Add crushed peppermint sticks and combine. If mixture is too thick or isn't mixing well, add a little hot water and stir. Add hot water and stir until mixture is moist and not runny. Once cream and peppermint is thoroughly combined, scoop onto cookies and replace tops.

Makes 32 cookies

> **DID YOU KNOW?** In Pensacola, Florida a burglar made off with a man's wallet, watch, and video game system. The burglar returned to the home later and snatched a 100-pound plasma-screen TV because the police left it in the victim's back yard, so they could come back and dust it for fingerprints.
> Source: *Sacramento Bee*, August 31, 2009

Chocolate & Peanut Butter Bowl

2 each plain chocolate candy bars
1-2 tablespoon peanut butter

Melt chocolate candy bars in their wrappers. Open and squeeze one candy bar into the lid of your hot pot and set aside until hardened. Scoop some peanut butter onto the chocolate and leave about 1/2 inch around the sides. Squeeze the other melted candy bar over the top and down the sides to cover the peanut butter. Set aside until chocolate is hard.

Serves: 1

> **DID YOU KNOW?** Texas has 112 prisons and employs 23,700 guards – which is 2,600 shy of the number authorized by the state legislature. The shortage of prison staff is not new and neither is the state's use of non-citizens as guards. The Texas Department of Criminal Justice (TDCJ) has a large number of immigrant employees, especially from Nigeria and Mexico.
> Source: *Prison Legal News*, June 2009

Chocolate Nutty Bar Cake

2 package nutty bars (crushed)	4 tablespoons hot chocolate mix
1 package chocolate crème cookies	4 each sweeteners
1/2 jar peanut butter	water

Separate fillings from cookies and set aside. Crush cookies. Mix the crushed cookies with the hot chocolate and sweeteners. Sprinkle with 2 teaspoons of water and press into large bowl. Then spread the peanut butter evenly over cake. Pour melted filling over the peanut butter and top with the crushed nutty bars.

Serves: 6

> **DID YOU KNOW?** Upon leaving their assigned jobs, inmates are required to strip, run their tongue around their teeth, open their mouth, stick out their tongue, lift up their breasts and stomach, squat and cough, turn around, lift their feet up, spread their butt cheeks apart, squat and cough again, lift their hands above their heads as they turn around, and finish by running their fingers through their hair.

Choc-O-Holic Delights

2 bags peanuts (crushed)	2 flour tortilla bags
1 bag chocolate covered peanuts (melted)	2 each plain chocolate candy bars (melted)

Mix in a large bowl the melted chocolate covered peanuts, chocolate candy bars, and peanuts. Form into 2 candy bars and wrap each bar in a flour tortilla bag. ***Devour slowly!***

Serves: 2

> **DID YOU KNOW?** On April 27, 2009, thirty prisoners at the Texas Youth commission prison in Crockett held a protest on top of the prison's gymnasium for several hours. Since the prison did not return media phone calls and reporters had no access to prisoners the reason(s) for the protests were not disclosed.
> Source: *Prison Legal News,* May 2009

CHOCOLATE PEANUT BUTTER CAKE

1/2 bag vanilla wafers (crushed)	3 each sweeteners
1 package double fudge cookies	1/2-3/4 jar peanut butter (melted)
3 teaspoons hot chocolate	chocolate syrup (desire amount)
1 each Milky Way candy bar (melted)	1 each Butterfinger candy bar (crushed)

Mix the peanut butter and vanilla wafers together and form the crust in a large bowl. Separate the cream filling from cookies and crush. Mix cookies with desired amount of chocolate syrup. Add the hot chocolate and sweeteners to the filling and pour over crust. Filling will be soft, but not runny. Melt the cookie filling and chocolate bar together and mix well. Then spread on top of cake. Sprinkle with the crushed Butterfinger candy bar.

Serves: 6

> **DID YOU KNOW?** Newly received inmates must wait six (6) months before they are eligible to be reviewed for a promotion in time-earning status.

CHOCOLATE PEANUT BUTTER CUPS

1 package peanut butter cookies
5 each plain chocolate candy bars

Remove the cream filling from cookies. Stack 2 or 3 of the filling discs on top of each other. Put chocolate bars in hot pot and let get warm but not runny. Clip a tiny corner of chocolate candy bar wrapper and squeeze from bottom, covering the peanut butter filling, stacked discs. Lift with spoon and put chocolate on bottom. Smooth with spoon. Let cool completely and eat. Tastes like you know who's peanut butter cups. ***Enjoy the taste!***

Serves: 6

> **DID YOU KNOW?** How heartbreaking it is to be separated from your family and loved ones for years? The suicide and attempted suicide rate among women prisoners are ever-increasingly high.

For The Sweet Tooth

CHOCOLATE PUDDING

| 3 packages powdered milk | For every pint of ice cream use 1 |
| 2 pints chocolate ice cream | 1/2 packages of powdered milk. |

Whip together until creamy and fluffy. The perfect PMS cure!
Serves: 4

DID YOU KNOW? The ten (10) people inmates are allowed to call in the free-world are taken from their approved visitation list.

CHOCOLATE RICE CRISPY CAKE

3 each rice crispy treats	1 1/2 cups hot chocolate
1 1/2 tablespoons peanut butter	chocolate syrup
8 each sweeteners	1-2 tablespoons butter
9 tablespoons water	1 1/2 package chocolate crème cookies

1. Remove chocolate chips from rice crispy. Cut rice crispy treats length-wise in half so you have 2 thin full size pieces.
2. Remove crème from cookies and crush cookies.

Add hot chocolate, 4 sweeteners and 9 spoons of water to crushed cookies. Mix well and press 1/2 cookie mix in a thin layer into a bowl. Place rice crispy treats shaped to cover the bottom of the bowl and slightly up the side. Mix peanut butter and chocolate syrup until creamy and easily spread over rice crispy treats and let set about 5 minutes. Add remaining cookie mix and press down until smooth. Mix cookie filling with butter and 4 sweeteners. You may need to add a few drops of water. Spread over cookies and sprinkle with chocolate chips.

Serves: 6

DID YOU KNOW? Inmates are only given 14 bars of soap every two weeks. Each bar of soap is about 1"x1/2"x1/8" and contains absolutely nothing to combat bacteria.

CHUCKLES

4 each Snickers candy bars	water
1 package double fudge cookies (crushed) (don't remove middle)	

Combine water with crushed cookies. Add enough water to make a moist paste. Shape in a bowl and pour melted candy bars on top. *Let set a few hours and enjoy!*

Serves: 4

> **DID YOU KNOW?** The Honolulu, Hawaii City Council is considering a bill that would impose up to a $500 fine and up to six months in jail for public transit passengers convicted of being too smelly.
> Source: *Sacramento Bee*, September 2, 2009

COCONUT CAKE

7-8 each macaroon cookies	1/4 cup powdered milk
1 package vanilla crème cookies	1 teaspoon butter
salt	water
8-10 each almonds from trail mix (crushed)	

Separate cookie filling from vanilla cookies. Crush 4 macaroons and the vanilla cookies together. Toss with enough butter to coat. Mix 1/4 cup powdered milk in hot water slowly to avoid lumps. Use to dampen crumbs. Press into bowl. Use more powdered milk and hot water so it makes about 2-3 tablespoons to mix with filling for frosting. Before frosting cake, crush 1 macaroon cookie and crumble on top of cake. Press into cake for crusty finish. Frost. Crush 1-3 macaroons coarsely. Mix with crushed almonds. Toss with a few drops of butter. Salt lightly and sprinkle on top of cake. Let set.

Serves: 6

> **DID YOU KNOW?** Death-row inmates are given the option of choosing to work in their dayroom. Their work consists of sitting in the A/C sewing craft items for the guards.

For The Sweet Tooth

COCONUT CHOCOLATE CAKE

1 package chocolate crème cookies	1 each plain chocolate candy bar
1 each Milky Way candy bar	5 each coconut and caramel candy
1/2 package coconut macaroon cookies	1 each Butterfinger candy bar

Separate cream filling from chocolate cookies. Melt fillings in container with coconut candy and chocolate bar. Keep hot. Crush macaroon and chocolate cookies to fine powder and mix together. Crush Butterfinger and blend into cookies, adding 1/2 spoonfuls of hot water at a time to make into "dough." Dough will be very sticky, but holds its shape. Press dough into large bowl or plastic tray from cookies. Spread hot cream filling mixture on top and let set. *Satisfying!*

Serves: 4

DID YOU KNOW? If it comes down to what an officer says happened, or what an inmate says happened – the officer is always right even if they're wrong!

CONFETTI CAKE

1 package double fudge cookies	1/2 cup hot chocolate mix
1 package M&M candy	1 tablespoon butter
1 package trail mix (take out the raisins)	water

Separate cookies from filling. Crush cookies. Toss crumbs with enough butter to coat. Melt 1/4 cup hot chocolate with hot water. Use just enough of this to dampen crumbs. Press into bowl. Use the rest of the hot chocolate to mix with the filling for frosting. Gently crush M&M candy pieces. Don't overdo it. You want to see color. Sprinkle on top of frosted cake. Crush nuts should be sprinkled evenly around candy pieces. Let set. *Yummy!*

Serves: 6

☺ **HELPFUL HINT!!** All cakes with 1 package of cookies will fill one cookie cereal bar container, plus one more row. We use a doughnut container or 2 small containers for extra.

CHOCOLATE COOKIE CAKE

1 package chocolate crème cookies	1 each cappuccino (any flavor)
2 each Snickers candy bars (can be Milky Way)	1/3 cup peanut butter
	1/4 cup hot water

Separate cream from cookies and put in small bowl. Crush cookies and separate cookie rounds so that half covers bottom of cake and half goes on top. Layer bottom of big bowl with cookies and add just enough of cappuccino mixture (cappuccino with 1/4 cup hot water) to make a wet but firm crust. Melt Snickers (or Milky Way) bar in hot pot. Put in small bowl. Add peanut butter to melted candy bar and stir. Add drops of water if necessary to make a thick paste. Do the same with cream from cookie (make paste with drops of water). Fold cream layer evenly over bottom crust in big bowl. Then fold chocolate/peanut butter mixture over it. Make final top layer with remaining cookie crumbs wet with cappuccino mixture. Spread evenly over top.

Optional: Garnish top of cake with crushed mint sticks, almonds, or chocolate.

Serves: 6

DID YOU KNOW? The keys for the inmate's locks may be kept on the ID chain (no yarn) or in their pockets. The key may not be carried in the metal clip on the ID holder.

COOKIE TWISTS

1 package cookies (any flavor)	3 tablespoons peanut butter (melted)
1 each chocolate candy bar (melted)	

In an insert mix the cream from the cookies with melted peanut butter and reassemble cookies. Drizzle with melted chocolate bar.

Serves: 6

DID YOU KNOW? Blow dryers and typewriters are allowed to be used in the bedroom area during the hours of 3:30 am until 10:30 pm.

For The Sweet Tooth

DEATH BY CHOCOLATE

1 package double fudge cookies	1 1/2 package powdered milk
1 pint rocky road ice cream	1/4 cup chocolate syrup
3 each chocolate Moon pies	

Mix melted rocky road ice cream and 1 1/2 packages of powdered milk in hot pot to cook for one hour. Crush up the package of chocolate fudge cookies in one bowl and in another bowl crush up the Moon pies. Layer the cookies, Moon pies, and ice cream mixture; top off with chocolate syrup.

Serves: 4

DID YOU KNOW? The female butchers are given men's metal gloves to wear for protection when operating the electric saws. The smallest size is a men's medium, and these are too big for the female inmates that have small hands.

DELECTABLE BROWNIES

| 1 each Milky Way candy bars |
| 1 each brownie |

Break up 1/2 brownie and place in insert. Layer with 1/2 candy bars crumbled. Repeat with other half of brownie then top with the other ½ of candy bars. Let cook for 45 minutes. Serve warm.

Serves: 1

DID YOU KNOW? In a national survey of imprisoned criminals, Texas has gained a dubious new distinction: five of the ten prisons with the highest reported rates of rape are in Texas. Of these five, Mountain View Unit is the only female prison.
Source: *The Austin American Statesman*, March 28, 2008

Fantasy Fudge Cake

2 packages double fudge cookies	1/2 bottle chocolate syrup
4 each Milky Way candy bars	3 teaspoons hot chocolate mix
2 each plain chocolate candy bars	

Melt the Milky Way candy bars in hot pot but leave in wrappers. Break apart the chocolate candy bar and place in hot pot insert.

Separate the cream filling from the cookies and put the filling in the insert with chocolate and heat. Crush the cookie halves in a large bowl. Add the chocolate syrup to the cookies and mix well. Leave a little lumpy. Place 1/2 of the cookie mixture in another bowl and pack down.

Spread the 4 Milky Way candy bars over the cookies and then top with the other 1/2 of cookies. Pack down evenly and set aside.

Add a small amount of water to the filling, keeping the consistency thick. Add the filling mixture on top and spread.

Serves: 6-8

DID YOU KNOW? Inmates are not allowed to go to the pill-line before going to the chow hall for breakfast or dinner.

Frosted Shredded Wheat Surprise

2 cups frosted shredded wheat cereal	1 each sweetener
1 tablespoon powdered milk	water
1 tablespoon banana whey	

Mix powdered milk, banana whey, and sweetener in insert with cold water. Put frosted cereal in bowl and pour milk mixture over. *Yummy!*

Serves: 1

DID YOU KNOW? Each year, tons of unused pharmaceuticals are flushed by America's state and federal prisons, hospitals, and long-term care facilities contaminating the nation's drinking water.
Prison Legal News, April, 2009

Fruit Cakes

1 package trail mix	1 tablespoon peanut butter
1 tablespoon strawberry preserves	hot water
6 each chocolate chip, coconut or oatmeal cookies (crushed)	2 packages instant oatmeal (any flavor)

Using an empty jar or hot pot insert, add first three ingredients plus about 1/4 cup hot water (not too much, you don't want it runny). Add the trail mix and stir well. Add 1/2 the crushed cookies and mix well. Add the rest and mix again. Let mixture set for six to eight hours. Drop the container in a hot pot and heat. Enjoy with a hot cup of coffee, cocoa, or tea.

Serves: 2

> **DID YOU KNOW?** Inmates eat their food directly off their plastic tray with a plastic "spork." The "spork" is a combination of a spoon and fork. Inmates are not allowed to use plastic knives, but they aren't sure why this is?

Girly Scout Cookies

4 each plain chocolate candy bars	2 each mint sticks
1 package chocolate crème cookies	water

Start early. Crush mint sticks and melt in hot pot insert. Use a scant spoonful of water. Don't put the lid on the hot pot. Cover with your cell towel so it does not "sweat." Leave heating all morning, stirring during commercial breaks.

Separate cookies from filling and beat the fillings into the melted peppermint. Then spread on the back of cookie and top with another cookie. Melt the chocolate bars and spread on each cookie. ***Mmm Mmm Good!***

Makes: 32 cookies

> **DID YOU KNOW?** Inmates are not allowed to ask their family or friends for money.

For The Sweet Tooth

GRASSHOPPERS

1 package double fudge cookies	1 each mint stick
1 each plain chocolate plain bar	

Separate double fudge cookie from filling and place cookies in a bowl and crush. Place filling into an insert cup. Add water to cookies to make a crust. Cook filling and chocolate bar; top crust with mixture. Crush mint stick and sprinkle on top.

Serves: 6

> **DID YOU KNOW?** Some dogs chase cars. A pit bull in North Carolina chomped into the tires of a deputy's cruiser causing all four tires to go flat. Source: *Sacramento Bee*, September 2, 2009

HALLOWEEN CAKE

1 each orange soda	1/2 cup hot chocolate mix
6-8 each orange slice candies	2 teaspoons butter
1 package chocolate crème cookies	

Dice the orange slices with the edge of ID card or protractor and put in your insert. Add about 1/4 inch of orange soda. Heat for about one hour stirring often, then drink the rest of the orange soda because kids in 3rd world countries don't get orange sodas.

Separate cookie from filling and crush cookies. Make chocolate syrup by mixing 1/2 cup of hot chocolate with hot water, but not a thick syrup with this cake.

Toss crumbs with enough butter to coat. Press lightly into bowl. Let cake set while cooking the orange slices.

After one hour, beat the orange slices with the cookie filling. It will still have a few lumps of candy, but that's okay. Frost the cake. Let set several hours before slicing.

Serves: 6

> **DID YOU KNOW?** It is the responsibility of the inmate to know and be aware of all prison rules, regardless of when they were made.

Ice Cream Cheese Cake

1 package cookies of your choice	water
2 bags powdered milk	2-3 each drink mix (any flavor, but make sure the flavor goes with the ice cream you choose)
1 pint ice cream of your choice (melted)	

Remove the cream from cookies and set aside. Crush cookies and add water. Add enough to water to where the mixture is pasty but not too moist. Mold into a pie crust in bowl. In separate bowl, pour melted ice cream. Slowly add powered milk and stir while pouring. Once you finish adding first bag of powdered milk, add the second while stiring. Remember to pour slowly while stirring, otherwise you'll have lumps. Slowly add drink mix while stirring. Once the mixture is sweet, pour your mixture onto the crust you made. Let set covered for about 6 hrs. Once hardened, add melted chocolate, melted centers of cookies, nuts, crushed cookies, candy, or anything else of your choice to the top. Cut and serve. *Yum!*

Serves: 4-6

> **DID YOU KNOW?** All inmate correspondence (except legal and media mail) is subject to being read by the mailroom staff (both incoming and outgoing) and possibly photocopied.

Ice Cream Chocolate Crunch

2 each crunch chocolate ice cream novelty (desired flavor)	8 each chocolate chip cookies or desired large cookies

Divide the ice cream novelty in half and sandwich between two chocolate chip cookies.

Serves: 4

> **DID YOU KNOW?** Detroit has battled crime for decades. The city had 375 homicides in 2008 and 379 in 2009. So far this year (2010), the number of homicides is down by about 34 over this time in 2009.
> *The Associated Press* by Corey Williams & Jeff Karoub May 21, 2010

Ice Cream Parfait

1 package double fudge cookies	1 1/2 package powdered milk
4 each lemon drink mix	1/2 bottle butter
1 pint ice cream (vanilla, strawberry-vanilla, or lemon swirl)	

Crush cookies till very fine then add butter to mixture. In a separate bowl, add melted ice cream, powdered milk and drink mix. Mix until thick. Use 2 inserts and starting with cookie mixture layer insert with cookie mixture, then the ice cream mixture alternating until you reach top of each insert.

Instead of inserts, you can also layer in white bowl. Garnish with anything sweet.

Serves: 4

> **DID YOU KNOW?** The dayroom capacity is clearly painted on the wall of the dayroom as 28. But, the seating available actually only accommodates 26 inmates and the dorms house 34 inmates. TDCJ also requires all inmates to be seated while in the dayroom. No exceptions.

Ice Cream Pudding Cone

2 each plain chocolate bars	1 package powdered milk
4 each cookies and cream ice cream cone	

Remove ice cream from cone without breaking the cone. In a large bowl, mix together ice cream with chocolate coating, one melted chocolate bar, and enough powdered milk until desired consistency. Whip until creamy and chocolate coating has dissolved. Place pudding back into saved cone shell and drizzle melted chocolate bar on top of each cone.

Serves: 4

> **DID YOU KNOW?** Why do our Arizona prisons remain immune from scandal? I don't mean that scandals don't happen, but that they don't seem to attract attention.
> *The Mesa Tribune*, August 11, 2008

Ice Cream Sandwich Cakes

| 2 each crunchy chocolate ice cream novelty (desired flavor) | 4 each oatmeal crème pies |

Divide the oatmeal pies in half. Place half of the ice cream novelty between the two halves and sandwich together.
Serves: 2

> **DID YOU KNOW?** At full staff, Texas prisons should have about 24,000 guards.
> Source: *The Houston Chronicle*

Lemon Coconut Bars

1/4 cup powdered milk	1 teaspoon butter
1 dash salt	water
1 package trail mix (minus the raisins)	2-4 each macaroon cookies (save container)
1 package lemon crème cookies (save container)	

Separate cookies from filling. Crush cookies. Set aside 1/2 cup of these crumbs. Toss crushed cookies with butter to coat. Add hot water to dampen crumb. Press into cookie containers.

Melt powdered milk with butter and hot water to make about 1/4 cup. Beat well with cream filling to make fluffy frosting.

Crush nuts from trail mix and toss with the remaining crumbs. Toss with small drops of butter and add a pinch of salt. Sprinkle over the top of frosted cake to form a crumb topping.

Serves: 6

☺ **HELPFUL HINT!** We like to add a dash of salt to the frosting, too. Leave the sunflower seeds in the nut mixture because they are a perfect compliment to lemon.

> **DID YOU KNOW?** When an inmate is talking to staff they are not allowed to be seated. They must stand.

Melt In Your Mouth Frosting

Top your favorite cookie, cake, or make a simple cookie fun.

Coco–nut Crunch: In an insert mix the cream from 1 package double fudge cookies, 2-3 tablespoons hot chocolate, 1-2 crushed Chick-O-Stick (or 1/2 to 1 Butterfinger candy bar) and desired amount of warm water. (any flavored cookie cream)

Nutt-illa Crème: In an insert mix the cream from 1 package vanilla crème cookies with desired amount of melted peanut butter.

Nutty Chocolate Crème: In an insert mix 1-2 tablespoons melted peanut butter with the cream from 1 package of double fudge cookies.

Smooth Chocolate Crème: In an insert mix with 1 melted chocolate bar with the cream from 1 package of vanilla cream cookies.

Sweet Strawberry Crème: In an insert mix with the cream of 1 package strawberry cookies; a few splashes of strawberry soda or a few splashes of strawberry/kiwi juice.

Tooth-aching Chocolate Crème: In an insert mix the cream of 1 package double fudge cookies, 1 melted chocolate candy bar or 1 package melted chocolate covered peanuts.

> **DID YOU KNOW?** Almost all Texas inmates do not get paid for working, their labor is free.

Milk & Honey Surprises

| 1 each Milky Way chocolate candy bar | 1 each Honey Bun |

Open up the Honey Bun package. Slice the Milky Way candy bar long ways in half and slip it into the package with honey bun. Heat in insert for 30 minutes. *Delicious!*

Serves: 1

> **DID YOU KNOW?** The inmate's clothes are all white so they are easily visible to the guards.

For The Sweet Tooth

Mini Ice Cream Sandwiches

1 package cookies of your choice
1 pint ice cream of your choice

Scoop middle of cookies out and use in another recipe. Place spoonful of ice cream onto cookie halves. Top with second cookie half.
Makes 32 cookies. ***Enjoy!***

> **DID YOU KNOW?** Inmates released on parole or mandatory supervision must serve the rest of their sentence day for day, under the supervision of a parole officer. For example: If an inmate has been sentenced to TDCJ for 10 years and is paroled after serving three calendar years, the inmate will be on parole for seven calendar years.

Mini Popcorn Balls

5 each Snickers candy bars	4 each M&M candy (plain)
1 cup hot chocolate mix	1 sleeve graham crackers
1/4-1/2 cup hot water	1/2 cup melted butter
1 bag popcorn	

In large bowl, crush the Snickers and M&M candy. It's easier to crush the Snickers if you tear into pieces before putting in bowl. Stir the hot chocolate into the crushed candy. Crumble the graham crackers into mixture, making sure the majority of the pieces are no smaller than about the size of a thumbnail. Add the hot water and mix thoroughly. Add the popcorn and mix well while coating the mixture with the melted butter. Make into little balls.
Serves: 8

> **DID YOU KNOW?** The psychology of criminal conduct (PCC) emerged as the brainchild of Canadian Researcher Don Andrews in the 1980s, and is based on 7 essential criteria: (empirical, ethical, practical, criminal covariates, social learning, explanatory models, and individual differences) -- www.insideprison.com

Mint Chocolate Cake

1 package chocolate crème cookies	3 each peppermint sticks (crushed)
2 each plain chocolate candy bars	hot water

In an insert, combine cream fillings with the two crushed peppermint sticks. If mixture is too thick or hard to stir, add a little hot water and mix well.

In a bowl, add water to crushed cookies to make a thick mixture. Remove half of the mixture and set aside in separate bowl. Spread remaining mixture in bowl. Pour cream mixture on top and spread. Add remaining cookie mixture and spread. Pour melted chocolate on top and spread then sprinkle remaining peppermint.

Serves: 6

DID YOU KNOW? Chief Justice for the Third Court of Appeals, Kenneth Law took two years to decide that money laundering is okay as long as you use checks and not cash.
Source: *Courts on Fire*, October 13, 2008

Mint Cookie Chocolate Drops

5-7 each plain chocolate candy bars (save wrappers)	2 each mint sticks (crushed to powder)
1 package chocolate crème cookies	

Melt chocolate bars in an insert. Separate cream filling from cookies. Filling will not be needed for this recipe. Crush cookies into pea-size, or smaller chunks. Add powdered mint sticks to melted chocolate. Heat and stir until melted. Fold into cookies, mixing well. Drop by spoonfuls inside of candy wrappers. Let set until candy can be removed without sticking.

Serves: 6

DID YOU KNOW? If you come into the system with a college education then you are barred from taking any vocational classes that TDCJ offers the inmates.

For The Sweet Tooth

Mint Delights

1 package chocolate crème cookies	4 teaspoons powdered milk
3 each plain chocolate candy bars	water
5 each mint sticks	

In a plastic insert, put about 1/2 inches of water and add the 5 broken mint sticks. Cook in hot pot until melted, about 5 hours. Take out any remaining pieces of candy. Stir in powered milk until creamy. Separate cookies, putting the cream filling in with the melted mint stick and mix completely. Melt candy bars in another hot pot insert. Spread filling on cookies bottom and replace with cookie top. Spoon chocolate on top and spread. Let harden for 2 hours.

Serves: 6

> **DID YOU KNOW?** Female inmates are given only 6 tampons every month.

Mississippi Mud Brownies

1 package chocolate crème cookies	4 each Snickers candy bars
3 chocolate or vanilla Moon pies	2 cups hot chocolate

Remove cream filling from cookies and put cream in an insert with the marshmallow layers from Moon pies. Add one spoonful of water and heat in hot pot while crushing cookies. Add one cup hot chocolate to crushed cookies, 1/2 hot pot lid of water and two of the candy bars – mashed until well blended. Cook mixture for 30 minutes.

Spread brownie in bowl. Layer melted marshmallow mixture on top.

Melt in insert the two smashed candy bars with one cup dry hot chocolate and 1/4 hot pot lid of water. Spread on top of marshmallow layer.

Serves: 6

> **DID YOU KNOW?** Inmates are not sold computers and they have no access to using the internet. However, inmates can buy a typewriter for personal use for $225.

MISSISSIPPI MUD CAKES

1 package double fudge cookies	3/4 cup hot chocolate
1 package trail mix (just nuts)	2 teaspoons butter
1 each chocolate Moon pie	water

Separate cookies from filling and crush cookies. Put the filling in insert and heat. It needs to be as hot as possible for frosting.

Separate marshmallow pie layers and scrape as much of crumbs as possible from the marshmallow layers. Melt the hot chocolate in a small amount of hot water – enough to make ½ cup of syrup. Toss the cookie crumbs in enough butter to coat. Add syrup to make the cake and press into a bowl.

Pinch marshmallow into small pieces and drop evenly over top of cake. Make another 1/4 cup chocolate syrup to add to the heated filling for frosting. Keep hot until ready to drizzle over marshmallow on top of cake. Even out with back of spoon. Top with crushed nuts.

Serves: 6

DID YOU KNOW? Since August 23, 1992, Anthony Graves has been behind bars for the gruesome murder of a family. There was no clear motive, no physical evidence connecting him to the crime.
Texas Monthly, October 2010, by Pamela Colloff

OATMEAL/PEANUT BUTTER COOKIES

5 packages plain oatmeal	5 each sweetener
1/2 cup peanut butter	1/4 cup water

Mix all ingredients together in a bowl. Divide into 6 balls of cookie mix and place on empty chip bag. Flatten cookies into 1/2 inch thickness. Let stand 3 hours until firm.

Serves: 6 cookies

DID YOU KNOW? Postage stamps are the free-world equivalent of money in prison.

Peach Pie Crunch

4 each peach pies	1/2 package vanilla cookies
1-2 tablespoon butter	3 packages cream cheese

Crumble peach pies, butter, and cream cheese in an insert and cook for 1 hour. Pour into a bowl and top with crushed vanilla cookies.

Serves: 4

DID YOU KNOW? Murderer Donny Johnson was recently sanctioned by prison officials for creating and selling post-card size paintings made with brushes fashioned from his own hair and ink lifted from M&M candies. He lives in the administrative segregation unit at Pelican Bay, confined to an 8x12 foot cell 23 hours a day.
Associated Press Newswire 4, August 2006

Peanut Butter Brownie Cups

1 jar peanut butter	1 cup hot chocolate
1 package double fudge cookies	1 bottle chocolate syrup
1 package chocolate covered peanuts	water

Remove cream from cookies and place in your insert. Crush cookies and mix with chocolate syrup and hot chocolate and 1/2 - 3/4 hot pot lid of hot water. Cook for 30 minutes in hot pot. Add peanut butter to cream filling and melt together, mixing well.

After cooking for 30 minutes form miniature cups. Fill cups with peanut butter mixture. Top cups with melted chocolate covered peanuts.

Serves: 6

DID YOU KNOW? Of the 32 states or jurisdictions around the world that have legislation allowing capital punishment for drug offenses, China, Iran, Saudi Arabia, Vietnam, Singapore and Malaysia are most committed to the practice.
The Associated Press by Veronika Oleksyn, May 17, 2010

Peanut Butter Granola Balls

2 packages brown sugar oatmeal	2 packages plain oatmeal
3 tablespoons peanut butter	2 tablespoons cold water
1 package trail mix or any mix	2 tablespoons hot chocolate mix

Mix all ingredients and add enough water so that you can roll into about 10 same sized balls. Roll each ball in hot chocolate powder.

Serves: 2

> **DID YOU KNOW?** Tougher rules and longer sentences mean that prison for white-collar inmates is no longer Club Fed.
> american.com, May 16. 2007

Peanut Butter & Jelly Pie – The Old Standby

1 jar peanut butter	1 bottle strawberry preserves
1 sleeve graham crackers	1/2 bag vanilla wafers
1/4 cup butter (melted)	1 each Sprite/7-Up soft drink
4 packages cream cheese	2 each Chick-O-Sticks (or 1 Butterfinger candy bar)
2 each plain chocolate candy bars	

1. Crust: In a large bowl, crush the graham crackers and half of the vanilla wafers and mix thoroughly. Add the melted butter a little at a time to make the crust and form to the bottom and sides of the bowl.
2. Filling: Mix the cream cheese with the strawberry preserves and pour into crust. Top with a layer of whole vanilla wafers.
3. Topping: Mix the peanut butter with enough Sprite a little at a time to spread smoothly over the vanilla wafers.
4. Melt the chocolate bars and pour over the top.
5. Sprinkle the Chick-O-Sticks on top so it will harden with the chocolate.
   Serves: 6

> **DID YOU KNOW?** If you are on cell restriction, you can only buy stamps once every 30 days. An inmate may have no more than 60 stamps in their possession at any given time.

QUICK CHEESECAKE FOR ONE

1 sleeve graham cracker (all 4 rectangles)	1 package single serving cream cheese
1 bottle strawberry jam	

Spread cream cheese on graham cracker and top with strawberry jam. All the taste without all the work!

Serves: 1

> **DID YOU KNOW?** The 9th Circuit Court, often in error but never in doubt, provides the Supreme Court with steady work: Over the last half-century, the 9th has been reversed almost 11 times per Supreme Court term, more than any other Circuit Court.
> *Ventura County Star* by George Will – May 20, 2010

REAL STRAWBERRY CHEESECAKE

15 packages cream cheese	1 bottle strawberry preserves
2 packages powdered milk	2 tablespoons butter
1/2 package lemon-lime sports drink mix	1/4 each Sprite/7-Up (softdrink)
1 package vanilla cream cookies (crushed)	

Crust – Crush cookies leaving in filling in a large bowl. Then mix in butter to form to bottom and sides of the bowl.

Filling – In bowl, mix cream cheese and strawberry preserves until creamy. Then add powdered milk, sports drink mix, and sprite. Whip it until it's fluffy and thickened. Pour over crust and let set for at least 2 hours.

VARIATION: Can use grape jelly in place of strawberry preserves.

Serves: 6

> **DID YOU KNOW?** Inmates are issued 3 bras and 3 panties every 4 months. These underclothes are manufactured in third-world sweatshops, in countries such as Bangladesh and Haiti, where workers earn $1 a day, working 8 hours a day, 6 days a week.

Red Apple & Banana Cheese Cake

2 packages powdered milk	4 packages apple oatmeal
1 package lemon drink mix	1/2 each Big Red soft drink
1 cup vanilla wafers (crushed)	banana chips (from trail mix)

Pour crushed vanilla wafers in a bowl. Add very little water and stir, consistency should be firm. In separate bowl combine milk, apple oatmeal, and lemon drink mix. Pour small amount of Big Red while stirring continually until smooth, once smooth, pour over crust. Hydrate banana chips by pouring a little water over them in a bowl and let them set for a few minutes. Let the cake set 3-4 hours until firm. Slice and serve.

Serves: 6

> **DID YOU KNOW?** Inmates are not allowed to talk with the inmates that are serving the food or drinks in the chow hall.

Smores

1 package honey graham crackers (crushed)	4 each plain chocolate candy bars (melted)
4 each vanilla or chocolate Moon pies	

Melt candy bars and leave in wrapper. Place crushed honey crackers on bottom of insert. Remove middles of 2 Moon pies and layer on top of honey crackers. Pour 1/2 of the melted chocolate on top. Repeat with graham crackers, middle of Moon pies, and chocolate. Let cook 30 minutes. *Fun!*

Serves: 2

> **DID YOU KNOW?** On October 2, 2009, the Eighth Circuit Court of Appeals, sitting en banc, held that shackling a pregnant prisoner while she was in labor constituted cruel and unusual punishment in violation of the U.S. Constitution.
> *Prison Legal News*, April 2010

Strawberry-Vanilla Cheesecake

10 packages oatmeal pies	3 packages powdered milk
1 each Sprite/7-Up soft drink	1 each plain chocolate candy bar
1 pint strawberry-vanilla ice cream (melted)	1 each strawberry pie (filling only)

In large bowl, press oatmeal pies together for crust. In another bowl, place partly melted strawberry-vanilla ice cream and strawberry pie filling. Mix and chop any whole pieces of fruit. Add 1 package of powdered milk and 2 or 3 teaspoons of Sprite. Mix well. Repeat with milk and Sprite until consistency is thick and creamy. Pour into oatmeal crust. In hot pot melt candy bar still in wrapper. Open and drizzle onto cheesecake. Take spoon and swirl. Let set overnight for best results, but can be eaten in 3 to 4 hours if you can't wait.

Serves: 6

DID YOU KNOW? In Texas, hanging was the means of executions between 1819 and 1923. From 1923 to 1981 it was electrocution; now it is death by lethal injection.

Swindler's Cups

1 sleeve snack crackers	1/2 cup peanut butter
2 each plain chocolate candy bars	

Add peanut butter and one square of chocolate bar to snack cracker and top off with another snack cracker. Great snack! Guess what candy bar it tastes like?

Serves: 2

DID YOU KNOW? In Ferndale, Michigan police say a first date went from bad to worse when a Detroit man skipped out on the restaurant bill, then stole his date's car. The man told his date that he had left his wallet in her car and asked for the keys. He then sped away in her vehicle.
Source: *Sacramento Bee*, August 31, 2009

TIRA MISU CHOCOLATE

2 pints chocolate ice cream	3 packages powdered milk
4 packages powdered donuts or chocolate cupcakes (broken up)	

Melt ice cream and mix in powdered milk. Stir until thick and creamy. Layer donuts or cupcakes upright around a bowl then pour chocolate mixture in. ***Yum! Yum!***
Serves: 4
VARIATION: May substitute ice cream with vanilla or strawberry.

> **DID YOU KNOW?** Harris County, Texas may lead in the number of people put in prison using questionable evidence. Evidence processed by the HPD Crime Lab – DNA, ballistics, drugs, whatever – must be considered questionable until and unless it can be retested by a qualified lab. There is no question that people were wrongly sent to prison by Harris County Courts.
> Source: *The Houston Chronicle*, March 28, 2003

TREE BARKS

2 packages maple brown sugar oatmeal	5-8 tablespoons hot chocolate mix
3-4 tablespoons peanut butter	4-5 tablespoons water
1 bag peanuts (optional)	1/4 cup butter

In a large bowl, mix oatmeal with melted butter, add hot chocolate and mix until the oatmeal is well covered. Mix in peanut butter. Use two spoons to smash and mix together with water until well mixed. Form into a long brick and slice with an ID card.
Serves: 10 slices

> **DID YOU KNOW?** In nearly all Dallas County cases, witness misidentification was an important factor in the conviction of the innocent defendants.
> *The Association Press* by Jeff Carlton

Very Berry Cobbler Parfait

1 pint. blueberry cobbler ice cream	3 insert cups
2 each cherry or strawberry pies	1 package powdered milk

In a large bowl, mix ice cream with powdered milk until creamy and fluffy. Crumble pies into small pieces. Layer the ice cream filling and crumble pie in the inserts. ***Scrumptious!***

Serves: 3

> **DID YOU KNOW?** The average time an offender remains on death row prior to execution is 10.26 years.

When The Lock Box Is Empty Cake

1 package lemon crème cookies	1/2 cup strawberry preserves
2 teaspoons butter	1 dash salt
3-4 teaspoons strawberry/kiwi juice (heat in insert)	

    Separate cookies from filling. Crush cookies. Toss with enough butter to coat. Chop 1/4 cup strawberry preserves into crumbs. Add small amount of butter. Press into bowl. Mix the hot juice into lemon filling for frosting. Add a dash of salt and mix. Drizzle over cake or drop by spoonfuls to swirl into frosting. We like to sprinkle a few sunflower seeds over the top.

    Serves: 6

☺ **HELPFUL HINT!!** Save your paper bag from the commissary if you are a cake maker. After slipping the cake back into plastic cookie packaging wrapper then slide it into the paper bag and fold the end to seal. It keeps better this way.

> **DID YOU KNOW?** Texas does not rehabilitate their prisoners. Texas only houses their prisoners while they serve their sentence.

PRISON LINGO

ACROSS-THE-BOARD – Punishment consisting of cell, recreation, and commissary restrictions – all at the same time. (Sometimes property restrictions are included).

A.T.W. – (All the Way) – going home to the free-world.

BABY's DADDY – Name referred to the father of a child.

BAD ACTOR – An inmate who doesn't follow the rules.

BACK-IN-THE-DAY – Something that previously happened years before.

BIG DADDY – Name given to a stud broad girlfriend.

BIRD BATH – Washing off at the sink instead of taking a shower – also referred to as "ho" bath.

BIRTH CONTROL – State issued eye glasses.

BLADES – Razor blades that have been removed from the holder.

BLUEBIRD – Transportation bus for inmates.

BOND MONEY – Line class that prevents you from going to medium or closed custody.

BOX – Storage place under our bunk that is about 1.75 x 1.75 cubic feet.

BULL DAG – Homosexual relationship (female).

BUNKIE – Cell-mate or cubicle neighbor in a dorm.

BUMP IT UP – Move up (forward) in line.

BUMPIN' YOUR GUMS – Rambling and talking non-stop.

BURNIN' OFF – Walking away.

BUST YOUR FEET – Move around fast.

BUSTIN' 85 – Spending the maximum allowed to spend at the commissary all at one time.

CATCH-A-CASE – To receive a disciplinary write-up which can be minor or major.

CELL WARRIOR – The dominant cell mate.

CHAIN BAG – Prison suitcase. (It's really a mesh produce bag).

CHANNEL CHECK – Changing the television station being viewed, which is allowed one time every hour.

CHEWIN' – Eating food.

CHOKE ON IT – To grab your aggie (hoe) at the head, bend over, and chop grass in that position.

CHOP IT UP – To get to know someone.

CHOP ON IT – To cut the grass in front of you.

CODE 20 – Sex case.

COMING UP – Leaving cell-block and living with general population offenders.

COUNT TIME – No movement on unit while guards count all the inmates to verify that no one has escaped. Count occurs every 2-3 hrs.

COURTESY FLUSH – Being mindful of your stinky poop and flushing as you drop.

CRACK YOUR FACE – To bust your bubble or scandalous confrontation.

CROSSED-OUT – Snitched on.

CUT IT – Chop your grass on hoe squad.

DASHING – Throwing liquid at guard or another inmate (usually urine).

DAYS AND A WAKE-UP – However many days and the morning you wake up to be released.

DIPPIN' – Being nosey.

DON'T PLAY – Tell the truth.

DOWN FOR IT – Okay with something/in agreement.

DOWNSTAIRS – Administrative segregation (it's really ground level).

DRIVE ON – To keep going (by walking).

DRIVE UP (DROVE UP) – To arrive somewhere (usually to a unit).

DROP A FORM – To request assistance from staff by sending an I-60 request for assistance or an HAS-9 request for medical assistance.

DRY SNITCH – Indirectly snitching.

DUSTY – An inmate with poor hygiene and presents themselves sloppily.

EAR HUSTLING – Eavesdropping on someone else's conversation.

FEELING IT – Not in the mood.

FISHING – Make a line out of string, or torn up sheets, to get something you want from another inmate at another location.

FIVE-O – Prison guard.

FLAGS – Postage stamps.

FLASHIN' – I'M FLASHIN' ON YOU – To remember something someone did and to get onto them about it.

FLIP THE SCRIPT – Lost your temper.

FORM DROPPERS – Someone who drops forms (I-60) to ranking officers snitching on others.

FREE-WORLD – Life outside of the prison environment.

FRONT-OUT – Exposing personal business to embarrass the victim.

GET ON – Move along.

GET ON STAGE – Pull a stunt (usually receive a lay-in from work).

GET ON THAT STUFF – To drink coffee and get "wired" from it.

GET OUT OF MY CAR – Mind your own business; get out of my conversation.

GET OUT OF MY GRILL – Stop watching my mouth (reading my words).

GO HARD – Giving it 100% full effort.

GO HOLLYWOOD – Drama mama; acting out to make a statement.

GOIN' DOWN – Getting into trouble.

GOIN' FED – Going crazy (not a date with Britney Spear's ex-husband).

GOIN' HARD – Describing something that's good or someone doing good at something.

GOOSING - Fornicating.

GO PLATINUM – Let someone "have it" i.e.; cussing at them.

GOT MY HUSTLE ON – Washing or selling or working to obtain commissary.

HANDLE UP – To take care of business.

HEAD HIGH – To raise your aggie as high as your head.

HO BATH – (bird bath) – a wash off in the sink instead of taking a shower.

HOE SQUAD – Group of inmates that work in the fields (not prostitutes).

HOLD WHAT YOU'VE GOT – Stop what you're doing and wait for further instructions or a "go ahead."

HOMIE – Friend.

HOOK UP – Write a case.

HOT SECOND – In a hurry, half a second.

HOUSE – The 6'x 9' living area of the inmate.

HOUSE MOUSE – "Domesticated" sugar mama/sugar daddy.

I GOT THAT – I have something that only 2 people know about.

INSTITUTIONALIZED – An inmate unable to function without the structure of the prison.

JAW JACKIN' – Talking non-stop.

JIGGERS – An inmate assigned to watch for prison guards (the lookout).

JOHNNIE – Brown lunch bag meal consisting of 2 sandwiches (one is always peanut butter and jelly).

KICKIN' IT – Hanging out.

KITE – Handwritten note to another inmate.

LACE HER UP – Giver the 411.

LAY-IN – A pass not to work or attend school due to medical reasons.

L.I.E. – Untruthfully reporting to the staff that an inmates life is in danger so the inmate can move to a different location.

LINE – The classification of an inmate.

LOCKDOWN – No movement on the prison grounds, all inmates are confined to their cells or cubicles.

MEAN MUGGIN' – Glaring angrily.

OFF PAPER/ON PAPER – Off parole/on parole.

OLD TIMER – Someone who has been locked up for a long time period.

ON EVERY SET – To do something every time you leave the dorm.

ON THE COOL – Trying to do something behind someone's back.

O.P. LIE – Request for inmate protection based on manipulation of the system.

OUT OF PLACE – Being some place without authorization.

PAPER – Receiving a disciplinary case.

PEN IN THE WIND – Writing a case.

PEOPLE – Homosexual couple.

PILL-LINE – Place where medication is issued to inmates.

PLAY CHILD – Unrelated inmate that is called "daughter" and this inmate calls her "mom." Ceyma is Celeste's play daughter.

PULLED UP – Just arrived on the unit or a specific location.

PULLING CHAIN – Moving off the unit to live on another unit.

PUT IT ON BLAST – To make something known to everyone/displaying someone's business.

QUICK MINUTE – Happening really fast.

RACK-IT-UP – All inmates report to their assigned house (i.e.; go to your cell/cubicle).

REC PANTS – The crotch is torn out so when the "people" are on the rec. yard, they can utilize the hole for their personal "recreational activity."

ROASTING – When an inmate verbally accosts another inmate in public or when the inmate is so upset; they are burning up with anger.

ROLL IT AROUND – The first person in the line walks around to end up behind the last person in line and everyone follows – making the last person first.

R.T.W. – Refusing to work.

RUNNING GAME – Form of manipulation (used on other inmates and guards).

SICK-CALL – Written request for medical attention.

SIGNING – To "talk" to another inmate without using your mouth, but using your hands to spell out words (prison sign language).

SHORT TIMING – getting close to being released from prison.

SHOT OFF – Moved/transferred to another unit.

SHOWING OUT – Purposely drawing attention in a negative way to oneself.

SIDE LINE – A second less important relationship.

SKIN IT BACK – Scraping grass with the aggie exposing dirt on the hoe squad.

SPIT BOXING – Arguing.

STATUS – Custody level.

STUCK-OUT – Left out.

STUD BROAD – Female inmate trying to look like a man.

THAT'S WHAT'S UP – That is the rumor.

THE BOMB – Outstanding.

THE GETTING PLACE – The black market.

THE RUN – The walkway or aisle between prison cells or cubicles.

THE STORE – Commissary; where the inmates buy food and supplies.

THROWED OFF - Crazy or insane.

THROWING LUGS – Making indirect derogatory remarks.

TOO THROUGH – Finished or fed-up with something.

TRICK – Sugar daddy or sugar mama.

WALK IT OFF – To go towards a destination.

WALLET – When inmates use their bra as a method of transportation.

WENT LEFT – Chewed someone out verbally.

WHERE YOU FROM? – Prison housing assignment not birthplace.

WIRED UP – Wearing a hidden electronic devise to tape record an officer or inmate.

Wounded Bird by Nancy Hall, is about Celeste Johnson's justice by terror in Texas after her husband was murdered. Wrongly convicted of conspiring with her husband's confessed murderer, Celeste's story is a must read for anyone wanting to understand how an innocent person gets trapped in the nightmare of being falsely accused and prosecuted for a crime he or she didn't commit. Includes letters from Gatesville Prison between Celeste and her mother Nancy Hall. 184 pages, softcover.

$15 (postage paid to U.S. mailing address)

Send check or money order to:
    Justice Denied
    PO Box 68911
    Seattle, WA 98168

Or order with a credit card from **www.authorhouse.com/bookstore**
To locate the book enter **Wounded Bird** in the search box.

Books published by The Justice Institute

Freeing The Innocent: How We Did It
By Michael and Becky Pardue

Michael Pardue walked out of an Alabama state prison in February 2001 after 28 years of imprisonment for three murders he didn't commit. Michael's wife Becky was instrumental in his exoneration. The Pardues decided to write a handbook explaining the tactics and strategies they used to overturn Michael's convictions.

Freeing The Innocent: How We Did It is the result of Michael and Becky's brainstorming. In their more than 50,000-word book, the Pardues cover what worked for them in four sections:

Part I covers what Becky and others did "On the Outside" to help free Michael.
Part II tells what Michael did "On the Inside" to help free himself.
Part III reveals how Becky's outside efforts and Michael's inside efforts meshed to help in fighting the system and winning.
The Appendix discusses legal aspects of undoing a wrongful conviction.

$15 (postage paid to U.S. mailing address)
82 pages, softcover

KIRSTIN BLAISE LOBATO'S UNREASONABLE CONVICTION

Possibility Of Guilt Replaces Proof Beyond A Reasonable Doubt

Kirstin Blaise Lobato's Unreasonable Conviction – Revised and Updated Second Edition

By Hans Sherrer

Kirstin Blaise Lobato was convicted and imprisoned for the July 2001 murder of a homeless man in Las Vegas, even though:

- There is no forensic, physical, eyewitness or confession evidence that either the 18-year-old Kirstin or her bright red car was at the murder scene, while fingerprints, DNA evidence and bloody shoeprints leading away from the body exclude her.
- On the day of the murder eleven alibi witnesses saw or talked with her in Panaca where she was living 170 miles north of Las Vegas.
- There is no evidence she or her car was in Las Vegas on the day of the murder.
- She was arrested based on third-hand gossip without any police investigation.

This revised and updated second edition includes information through September 2010, including a summary of Ms. Lobato's Nevada habeas petition that includes 24 grounds based on new evidence of her actual innocence.

Written by Hans Sherrer, editor and publisher of *Justice:Denied* magazine.

$12 (postage paid to U.S. mailing address)
174 pages, softcover

Kirstin Blaise Lobato vs. State Of Nevada
Compiled by Hans Sherrer & Michelle Ravell

Complete 770-page Nevada state habeas corpus petition filed with the Clark County District Court in Las Vegas on May 5, 2010. The petition's 79 grounds include 24 new evidence grounds; 2 *Brady* violation grounds; 52 ineffective assistance of counsel grounds; and 1 actual innocence ground.

Included is the press release about the filing of the petition, and a complete index of the petition to easily find each page referring to a particular topic.

Each ground is explained and supported by documentation and exhibits that include reports by forensic science, medical and entomology experts.

$20 (postage paid to U.S. mailing address)
792 pages, softcover

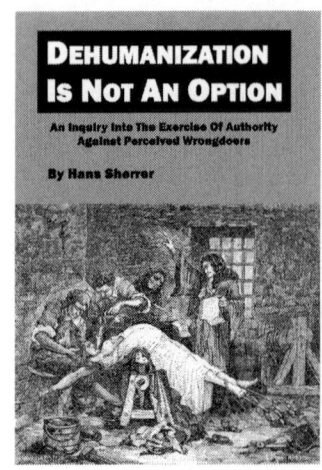

Dehumanization Is Not An Option
By Hans Sherrer

People around the world were shocked when gruesome details were revealed about the mistreatment of prisoners at Abu Ghraib, Guantanamo Bay and other detention facilities run by the United States. Yet their treatment in general differs only by degree from the treatment of people imprisoned in the U.S. and other countries.

This mistreatment is not due to the rogue actions of a few "bad apples." It is a predictable response by people placed in a position of authority over those they see as undeserving of humane treatment.

Dehumanization Is Not An Option explores how the inhumane treatment of real or suspected wrongdoers is contributed to by the unleashing of authoritarian attitudes, and that bureaucratic systems contribute to barbaric behavior.

Chapters include:
- Obedience To Authority Is Endemic
- Dehumanization Paves The Path To Mistreatment
- Psychological Dehumanization of Prisoners
- Bureaucracies Fuel Dehumanization

Written by Hans Sherrer, editor and publisher of *Justice:Denied* magazine.

$10 (postage paid to U.S. mailing address)
100 pages, softcover

From The Big House To Your House
By Ceyma Bina, Tina Cornelius, Barbara Holder, Celeste Johnson, Trenda Kemmerer, and Louanne Larson

Includes 200 recipes for easy to prepare meals, snacks and desserts. From The Big House To Your House has two hundred easy to prepare recipes for meals, snacks and desserts. Written by six women imprisoned in Texas, the recipes can be made from basic items a prisoner can purchase from their commissary, or people on the outside can purchase from a convenience or grocery store. Also included are many cost saving tips.

$14 (postage paid to U.S. mailing address)
132 pages, softcover

TO ORDER any of these books send a check or money order with complete mailing information to:

>Justice Denied
>PO Box 68911
>Seattle, WA 98168

Or order with a credit card from **www.justicedenied.org/books.html**

A catalog of dozens of books related to wrongful convictions, and legal and educational self-help that are sold by Justice Denied is available by writing:

Justice Denied
PO Box 68911
Seattle, WA 98168

Celeste Johnson

"Trial by Perjury"

Despite the protections from government abuse in the 5th and 14th Amendments, my trial proves that the government will misuse their duty to be fair, just, and proper when prosecuting people it knows to be innocent. My judge had no problem giving them a free pass to engage in these practices. Visit www.freeceleste.com to read about this incredible injustice.

www.freeceleste.com

Trenda Kemmerer

"Abuse of Power"

We are taught at an early age to honor the words in the "Pledge of Allegiance." Most citizens are raised with the illusion that in the U.S.A. there is JUSTICE FOR ALL. Justice in my case is what the State of Texas fabricated. Visit www.freetrenda.com for all the details.

www.freetrenda.com

Notes

Notes

Notes

Notes

Notes

Notes

Printed in Great Britain
by Amazon